Dᴇsɪɢɴ Yᴏᴜʀ Oᴡɴ Nᴇᴇᴅʟᴇᴘᴏɪɴᴛ

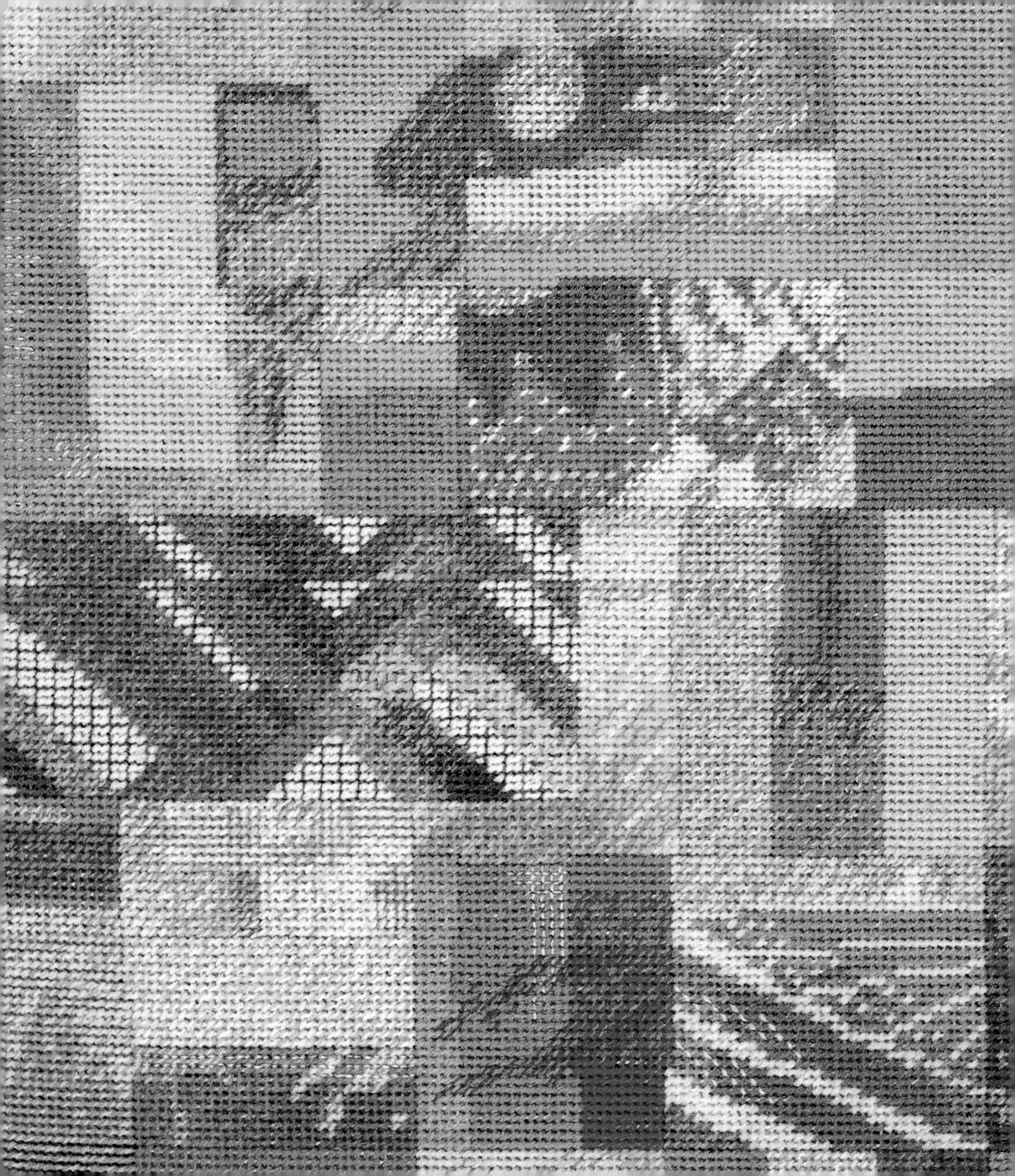

DESIGN YOUR OWN NEEDLEPOINT

Ann Gittins and Jennie Petersen

B.T. Batsford Ltd · London

ACKNOWLEDGEMENTS

The authors and publishers would like to thank the following: Kaffe Fassett for permission to reproduce his cow design and Sarah Windrum for permission to use her design 'Sheep at Cwmcarvan' (pp. 51–2), both published in *Noah's Ark: Animals in Needlepoint* by Hugh Ehrman and Elizabeth Benn; W.H. Smith & Son Ltd for the wrapping paper used in Chapter 5; the American Quilter's Society for Richard Walker's photograph of Jennie's quilt (p. 78); Andrew Lawson, whose photograph for the cover of the Royal Horticultural Society magazine *The Garden* was the inspiration for the embroideries in Chapter 8; the Japan Information and Cultural Centre at the Japanese Embassy in London for their help with the script for the Boys' Day card (p. 89); Irma Ernstsons, who has made up our cushions so beautifully; and, finally, those friends and relatives who temporarily returned the presents made for them so that they could be photographed.

First published 1995

© Ann Gittins and Jennie Petersen 1995

Typeset by Goodfellow and Egan Ltd, Cambridge

and printed in Singapore by Kyode

Published by
B.T. Batsford Ltd
4 Fitzhardinge Street
London W1H 0AH

A catalogue record for this book is available from the British Library

ISBN 0 7134 7379 7

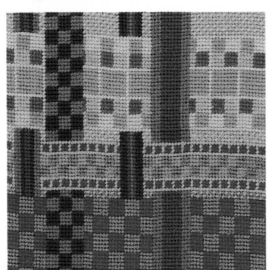

CONTENTS

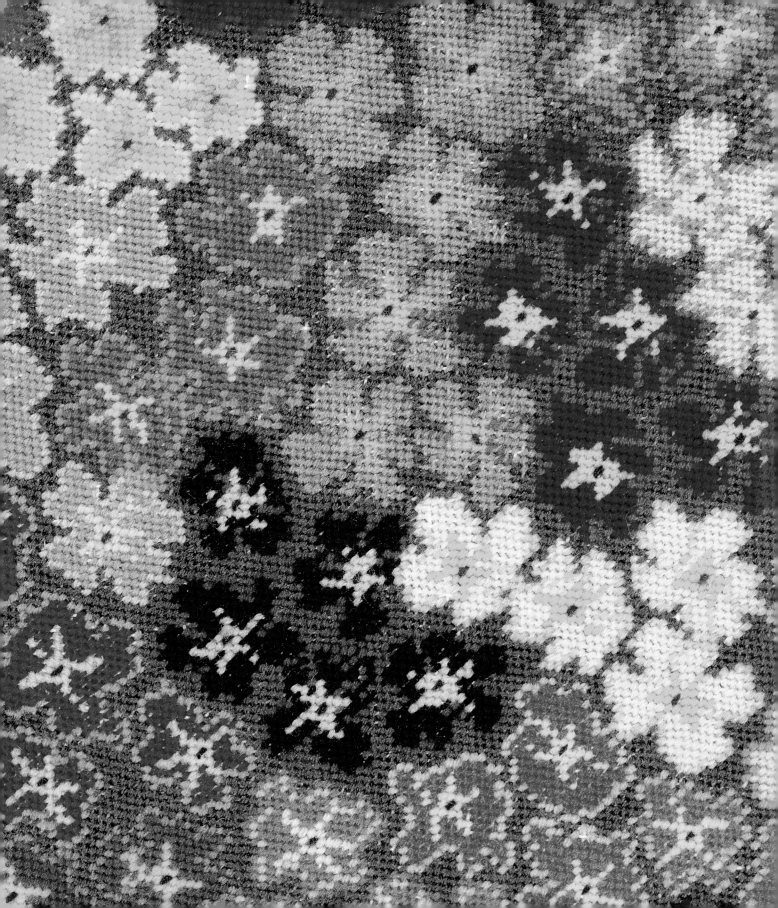

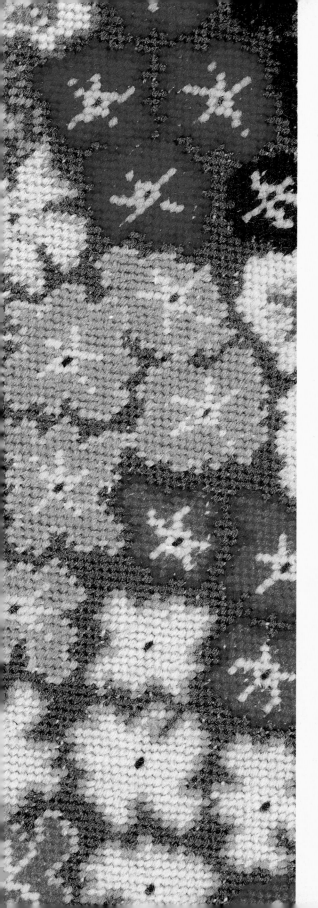

INTRODUCTION

This book has been written for people who enjoy stitching of any kind. We often meet them as we sit stitching on beaches, at airports, on trains and in hospitals. Most are surprised to find that we are not using commercial designs but are busy 'stitching our own thing'. Occasionally someone has even lifted our work up to see whether the design is printed on the back! We have had many enjoyable conversations about our designs and where they come from. On holiday abroad, our vocabulary was not always equal to the interest we provoked, and we had to resort to sign language. But, however we communicated, we found the message was the same. Most people said, 'I couldn't do that. I can't draw.' We replied, 'Neither can we.'

We do not profess to be experts. However, we do feel confident enough to design our own work and much prefer to do so. We hope in this book to help you increase your confidence in your own abilities by sharing some of the strategies developed during our long experience of creating individual pieces for our homes, families and friends. As former teachers we know that children can design with ease. The inhibitions that adults develop about their own efforts prevent many of them from taking the plunge and creating for themselves.

In this book we will try to help you release skills you may not have explored since primary school. Our aim is to encourage you to recapture the freedom and pleasure of childhood play, in which opportunities abound and established rules change as the players think up better ones. Working with canvas and threads is like painting. The principles are simple yet the variety you can achieve is far greater than anything derived from pre-designed commercial products.

A selection of our work is used in the book, both to illustrate the points we make and to demonstrate design possibilities. Our efforts are not bound by tradition or a particular view of the world, and our inspiration has come from both the mundane and memorable parts of our lives.

We hope very much that, as a result of reading this book and experimenting with some of our suggestions, your own ideas will blossom and give you pleasure and fulfilment.

CHAPTER I

BEING IN CONTROL

Commercially designed products are available in shops and by post from numerous outlets. Sold as kits, they vary in size and complexity. They are either printed on canvas in the prescribed colours or come with a chart showing the colour of each stitch. They are often boxed very attractively and usually include the necessary threads and even a suitable needle. Every needlework shop is packed with them and lots of people enjoy working them. Yet many of our friends have half-finished kits abandoned in cupboards, and one took twenty years to finish her first attempt! We believe that sewing your own designs is much more interesting than using kits, and has a number of other advantages which will be discussed in this chapter.

CUTTING COSTS

It is obvious to anyone who has bought a kit that they are very expensive. Buying the contents independently, as separate items, reduces the cost by about two-thirds. There are further ways to make savings, as later chapters of this book will reveal. The more needlework you do, the more materials you can collect for use in future projects.

Saving the pennies. An experiment using a technique seen on a piece of shisha mirror work from India. The coins were attached to the canvas with metallic thread

8

LEARNING

Kits usually include a set of instructions. Some are excellent guides, showing how to complete the work successfully. However, others are so over-simplified that they are ambiguous. Conversely, some kits are complicated and therefore discouraging, especially for a beginner. The colours printed on canvas may be difficult to distinguish and to match with the wools provided.

Designing is hard work and certainly taxes the brain. But working something out for yourself is very satisfying. You learn as you go along and sometimes find ways of tackling a problem you may not even be able to put into words. As a designer, *you* are in control.

9

PLEASING YOURSELF

The designs used in most kits are based on a limited range of cultural and historical sources. Traditionally designers have drawn inspiration from nature and from the creative efforts of previous generations, interpreting the work of well-known artists. These are 'safe' products for manufacturers to develop, safe because many people find them attractive. But they can be stuffy. Kits cannot meet all our cultural and personal preferences in terms of colour, pattern and imagery.

It is interesting to note how tastes have been shaped by the influence of large furnishing companies. These may inhibit us from exploring ideas that do not fit into their sanitised design styles, which can now be bought in whole roomfuls at a time. Our view of what we consider to be beautiful becomes limited. Designing for yourself makes you look for patterns and inspiration as you have never looked before.

EXCITING COLOURS

Using kits can restrict the colours in your work. Original designs often feature a multitude of colours, but to make a design commercially viable the number has to be reduced. Using fewer colours not only cuts the cost of production; it simplifies the design, making it easier to follow. Fine gradations of colour are difficult to produce in printed or chart form.

Colours used in kits tend to be those most likely to appeal to a large number of people. They would not necessarily be the first choice of each individual buyer. The 'average' view may be the least exciting possibility. Unusual colour combinations are unlikely to be available. Your personal designs can include colours as dark or light, vivid or subdued as you wish, with mixtures ranging from conventional and modish to eccentric and unfashionable.

BANISHING BOREDOM

One of the worst things about sewing other people's creations is the tedium of completing them. The only question to be answered is, 'Which bit shall I do next?' If, as you sew the design, you do not really like the effect, there is not much you can do about it. Children trying to copy an adult's drawing are often dispirited by the obvious difference between their efforts and the original. In the same way, when a relative beginner completes a design produced by a professional, the results are not likely to be as slick as the illustration.

The most important reason for working with your own ideas is that it is endlessly exciting. But be warned! Once you have taken to it you will become an addict. Your stitching will be a challenge, involving constant decisions. Instead of 'painting by numbers', you are an original artist. Colours, stitches, images, textures and patterns are controlled by you. By the time a piece of work is finished you will have made a huge number of decisions about it; you do not have to make them all at the beginning. You will probably change your mind as the piece progresses and may even undo some stitches or work over them to improve an effect. You will find yourself looking at your work more inquisitively than before. Since there is no precise picture on a package to show what the final result will be, your ideas may not be perfectly formed and will need checking as you go along. Looking sideways at your work, or scrunching up your eyes, or peering from different distances as ideas emerge will help you to see whether they are working.

TAKING TIME

If you are not already persuaded, you can add to the above points a feeling of pride in making something exactly as you want it; the satisfaction of creating personalised gifts ('Oh good, another heirloom!' one relative was heard to say); and the pleasure of seeing your ideas develop and improve as you experiment and learn by experience.

Everyone is capable of painting with threads on canvas. It is a leisurely process, giving you plenty of time to think as you work. The imagination expands with practice. In this book we explain some of the short-cuts we have found to give pleasing results. At the end of each chapter there is a project for you to try,

chosen to exercise your imagination and develop your design skills. Each project has a specific aim so that, if you try them all, you will build up a repertoire of strategies and techniques. As you work on them, be self-critical in a positive way. By voicing your doubts about something you give yourself the chance to find a remedy for it. It is no use simply saying, 'I don't like it.' Instead, try to identify the precise element that displeases you. For example, you may say, 'I don't like the dark colour behind the red.' You can then move forward. (The good news is that it is not always necessary to undo something completely in order to change it!) It is well worth taking time to make sure that you are happy with the result of your labours. The more you review what you do, the more flexible you will become about improving on your initial ideas. Remember *you* are in charge.

The look of a design depends on the colours you use

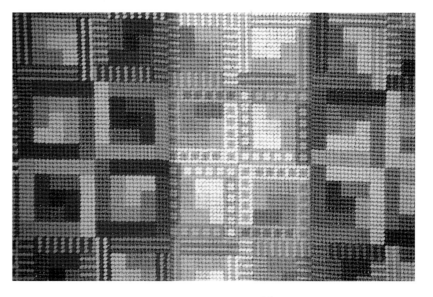

GREAT GRIDS

If you are a beginner read Chapter 3 first for basic instructions. If you are an experienced stitcher start here!

This is a project to help you begin to create your own designs. You could use it to make a pincushion. On a piece of canvas at least 15 cm (6 in.) square, mark a 10 cm (4 in.) square. Draw lines at irregular intervals down and across it to make a grid pattern. You may want to practice on graph paper first to find the pattern that pleases you best.

Choose a colour for the background with up to five other colours for the grid. You might choose a dark or light background and colours that are very different from one another, or shades of the same colour.

Work your first horizontal stripe (fig. 1A). Where it crosses a vertical stripe work alternate stitches only. Choose a different colour and work the second grid stripe in the same way (fig. 1B). When all the horizontal stripes are done, start on a vertical stripe. Where it crosses a horizontal stripe fill in the alternate stitches you left out before (fig. 1C). Complete the other vertical stripes using all your chosen colours. All that then remains is to fill in the background (fig. 1D).

If you have enjoyed this project you might like to use it to make a larger piece. You might prefer not to use a background and mingle all the stripes by working alternate stitches throughout to give a more tweedy effect. If you want to make a cushion you could use two different grid patterns, one for the middle and another as a border. You could make one of these grids of diagonal lines if you prefer. It is quite difficult to work diagonal grids but fun to try.

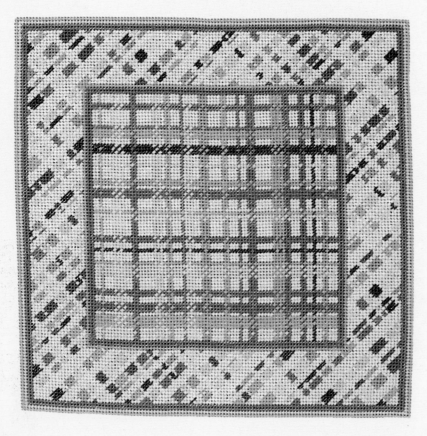

Great Grids

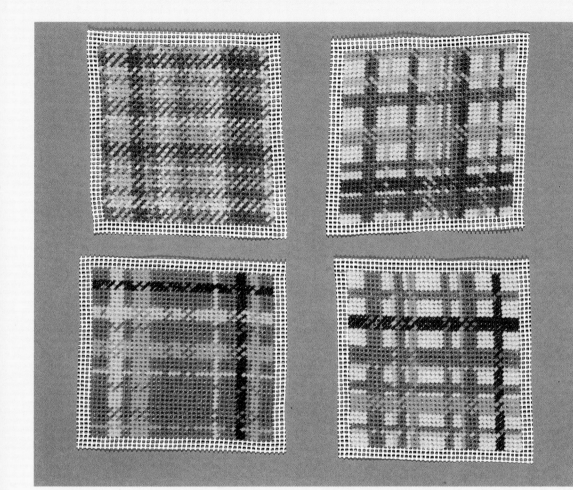

Working a series of
samples will help you see
the possibilities of this
exercise

Below: Fig. 1
A First horizontal
  grid stripe
B Second horizontal
  grid stripe
C First vertical
  grid stripe
D Completed grid with
  background

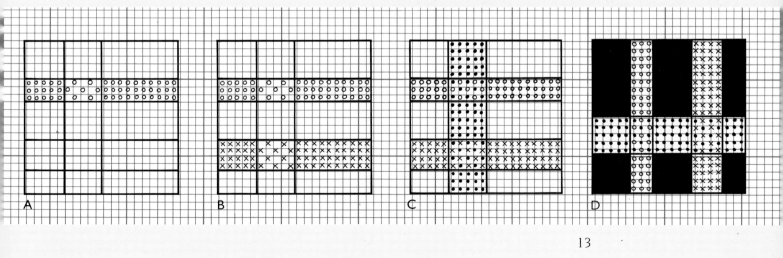

A   B   C   D

CHAPTER 2

LOOKING AND STORING

Where do your ideas come from? It is important to consider this question if you intend to create your own designs. We are told, although we may find it hard to believe, that absolutely everything we have ever seen is permanently stored in the brain, and the imagination simply reprocesses images from the past, which are then recycled, re-combined and re-formed. When we dream we combine fragments of experience effortlessly into rich and sometimes incongruous pictures, but it is not always easy to recall the details when we wake up. Can you remember your bedroom when you were seven or eight years old – the curtains, the furniture, how it was arranged? You probably spent many hours looking at it, but your memories may be hazy.

The design opposite was based on cuttings from magazines (below). Note how strange eyes look when divorced from faces!

It is interesting to revisit a place we knew well as children. It usually looks surprisingly small. This is evidence that the brain compares what is seen with the picture it has retained since childhood, supporting the theory that all experience is stored in the memory. This is wonderfully reassuring for would-be designers. It means you have a vast number of ideas waiting to be used. All you have to do is to take them out of storage. Unfortunately this is not as easy as it sounds. The older you are and the richer your supply of memories, the harder it becomes. How do you find what you want in such an abundant collection? Anyone who has used a computer knows that it is essential to put information into it in an orderly way if you want to find it again. The human brain is like a computer in this sense. It is easier to remember something if your brain knows, when you store it, that you are likely to need it in the future. If you want to become more inventive you will have to try to look at things around you more actively. This will warn your brain that you may want to use the images again.

Different people develop different ways of looking and seeing. In the following pages we shall discuss some of the methods we have found useful (and enjoyable).

15

PHOTOGRAPHY

Taking a photo of something that has caught your eye is a good way of studying it closely. You have to decide how to capture the essence of it, the quality that has attracted you. You have to frame it as you look through the viewfinder and decide what to include and what to leave out. Such thinking provides a strong warning for your brain that the image interests you and that you may want to explore it further. What is more, you will have the photograph to remind you of what you saw. Unless you are a very lucky or brilliant photographer, the print will not capture all that you remember, but it will act as a strong prompt to your brain. Sometimes the photograph will be easier to work with than the original because you have simplified the image by recording it in a rectangular frame. Sometimes you will accidentally produce something that adds a new dimension to your thinking. For example, a print that has been wrongly exposed or is blurred may give you unexpected inspiration and suggest colours or shapes you would not otherwise have considered.

If you come to enjoy photography with a designer's eye you will have to get used to people giving you strange looks as you zoom in on such things as an interesting rock formation, a tangled weed, a row of washing on a line, or shadows on a wall, while those around you are busy photographing each other or the eternal beauty of the sunset!

COLLECTING POSTCARDS

Choosing a postcard makes you concentrate on what you want to remember of what you have seen. You carry away a picture, as you do when you take a photograph, to remind you of what you liked about that particular view or building or work of art. You will remember things about it that the card alone cannot convey: its size and scale, its setting, its textures, the light in which you saw it, its overall impact.

Shadows make commonplace objects more interesting

Opposite: Arranging photographs to make a pleasing display gives an added dimension to the collection. The whole is more than the sum of the parts

17

DESCRIBING IMAGES

Talking about what you have seen is another way of fixing images in your brain. Searching for words to describe an image makes you focus your mind on it. The use of language increases the amount of information stored in your head about an experience, making it easier to capture the qualities of what you have seen when you try to recall it and work with it later. If you have been able to describe colours or textures or structures, you will find ways of echoing them in what you create.

LOOKING AGAIN

Gazing at something repeatedly will add to the image that your brain has already stored away. For example, you may walk the long way round to the shops just to look again at a beautiful tree that has caught your eye, and to engrave the sight of it on your mind. Viewing something from a different angle will also increase your understanding of it. Making a display of photos and pictures that reflect your current interests will help you to keep on looking and will add to the data in your brain. Just as seeing a film for a second time allows you to notice things you had missed before – a twist in the plot, a casual remark hinting at what was to happen later – so re-examining a visual image will reveal it to you in a new light, so that it may come to take on a new meaning.

COLLECTING CUTTINGS

Try browsing through old magazines and removing anything that catches your eye – an interesting juxtaposition of colours, a photo, sketch or cartoon. Poetry and prose can evoke particular memories, while old calendars, greetings cards or wrapping paper can also be added to the store of possible design sources. Pieces of fabric can suggest intriguing colour combinations and textures, and it is often worth keeping a scrap of an old, well-loved garment or a square of an unwearable creation that has caught your eye at a jumble sale.

RINGING THE CHANGES

It is fun to keep a notice-board or clip-frame to display some of your collection, and to change the pictures on it frequently. Arranging images and deciding which ones to put together can lead to unexpected connections and contrasts between shapes, styles and colours. The results can be very pleasing, too, and you can learn a great deal even from arrangements that you reject.

Other ways of experimenting productively include:

- Re-organising your collection by sorting it according to colour or subject matter.
- Weeding out those parts of your collection that no longer please or interest you.

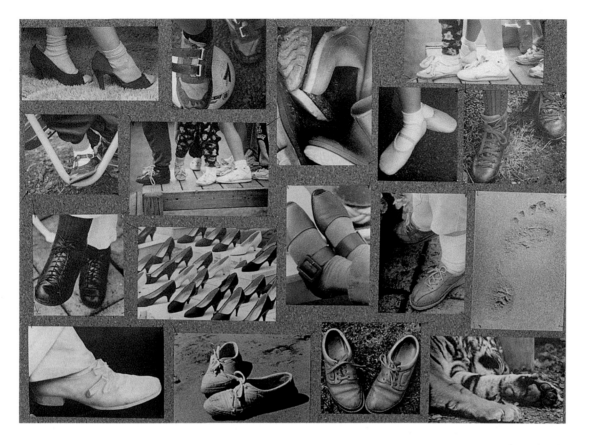

It's feet this week!

□ Searching for a specific image, e.g. a picture of a particular animal, which you might need for a design.

THE WORLD AROUND YOU

As you look more actively you will see more purposefully and your hunger for visual stimulation will grow. You do not need a lot of money or leisure time to be an active collector of visual experiences – there are possibilities all around you.

□ Have you looked recently at the buildings above your local shops? In many places they are surprisingly varied and interesting, and yet most people seldom lift their eyes to see

them. Markets, fairs, supermarkets and antique shops can also be fascinating visually. You can examine intricate details and notice, in contrast, the impact of large numbers of goods displayed together.

□ Make the most of daily chores. Have you ever looked carefully at cross-sections of vegetables or pieces of fruit as you slice them? How do the thorns grow on a rose stem? How do the patterns on a set of tiles fit together and repeat?

□ Set yourself tasks on the bus journey to work. Look at people's feet: the angle at which they are placed in relation to the leg; the way the shoe moulds to the shape of the foot. What deductions can

19

Children are closer to the ground than adults and often see things we do not notice

you make about a person simply by looking at their feet? Are your suppositions confirmed when you look at their overall appearance? Alternatively you might start by looking at people's heads. Try thinking of as many words as possible to describe their hair. Look at their hats.

□ There are endless natural sources of inspiration: plants and animals, the ever-changing sky, the effects of wind and weather, and so on.

□ It takes time and money to visit museums and art galleries, theatres and concert halls, but these can be real treats for the eyes, as can carnivals and parades.

□ Take a walk with a child. Children can teach adults a great deal about looking. They examine small things minutely and will talk excitedly about things you have grown to regard as commonplace. They ask questions all the time in order to link what they know with what they see. We all had such curiosity once and can discover its pleasures again.

PROJECT TWO

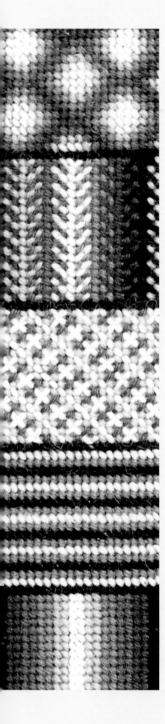

TONES ALONE

You can tell if a piece of fabric is textured by feeling it with your eyes shut. It will be rough. The aim of this project is to produce the illusion of texture by using stitches which are smooth but are worked in light and dark tones. It should also encourage you to look carefully at different textures and to think about how you can reproduce them in embroidery and incorporate them in your designs. You will need thread in four or five shades of the same colour. Choose the palest and darkest shades available and two or three tones in between.

Divide a piece of canvas into squares or rectangles with sides at least 5 cm (2 in) long. The total size will depend on what you want to make and on how many experiments you want to try. Each space will contain a different pattern. In the first four spaces try the four patterns shown below. When you have worked these, look at them from a distance. Do they look textured? Do they remind you of textures you have felt?

In the remaining spaces try some patterns of your own and attempt to produce the illusion of texture. When you become confident, you can try looking at different textures (knitting, dishcloths, woven fabrics or, more difficult, tree bark, leaves and bricks) and reproducing them in stitches.

Experiments with tone: try some of your own

21

CHAPTER 3

BEING PREPARED

EQUIPMENT

You must have the following:

☐ Canvas
☐ Threads
☐ Needle
☐ Scissors

You may also want to invest in a frame.

Canvas

Canvas comes in a variety of gauges (numbers of squares to the centimetre or inch) and is bought by the metre. As a rule it is more than 50 cm (20 in) wide. One metre (1 yard) will usually provide enough for several embroideries. We use canvas which has between 10 and 14 holes to 2.5 cm (1 in). Finer canvas is more difficult to see and takes longer to work, while coarser canvas is harder to cover and does not allow you to work small shapes accurately. Canvas is sold in two tones, light and dark. Use the lighter canvas if you are working a light-coloured design and the darker one

if your colours are predominantly dark. This will help prevent the canvas showing through the threads when the embroidery is finished. Canvas also comes in either single or double weaves. It really does not matter which you choose, although we find single-weave canvas easier to work.

Threads

Canvas is usually worked in wools sold specifically for the purpose: tapestry or tapisserie wool, Persian wool (which is stranded) and crewel wool (which is very fine). There are several manufacturers, and together they produce a fine palette of colours and shades, some only in small hanks, others in both small and large hanks. The large sizes are useful if a single colour is going to be a major feature of your design.

Crewel wool is often difficult to find, but it is worth searching out as it is marvellous for shading and also for stitching detail.

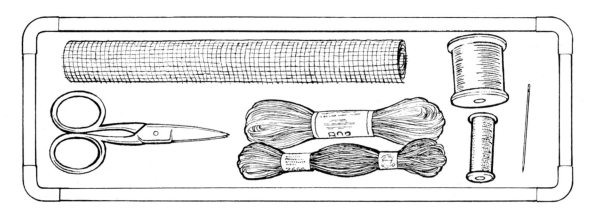

Fig. 2 Basic
equipment

22

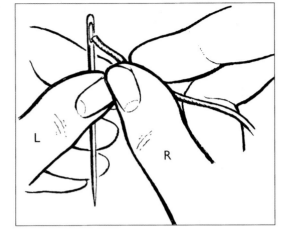

Fig. 3 *Do not try to thread the needle this way*

Needles

Use a short needle with a blunt point and an eye large enough to allow the wool to lie flat within it. Special tapestry needles are available in a range of sizes. The size of needle will depend partly on the gauge of the canvas you are using. The needle and thread must slip through the holes in the canvas easily and not be so big that the mesh is forced apart. Tapestry needles are easy to thread if you know the trick (see fig. 4).

Scissors

Any reasonably sharp scissors will be adequate but, if you do a lot of canvas work, you will probably want to buy some small embroidery scissors with sharp points.

Frames

Canvas is a stiff mesh of squared threads. As you use it, it becomes softened and will distort unless you attach it to a frame that maintains the rigid squareness of the fabric. It is perfectly possible to work without a frame, and you can have the finished work stretched back to the proper shape. However, if you use a frame you can sew with an even tension and the stitches will look smooth and regular. We think that this enhances the final effect. A frame seems unwieldy and you may feel clumsy at first, but you will soon learn a comfortable and quick way of sewing with the canvas held taut. It is rather like getting used to wearing a seat belt in a car. It seems restrictive at first, but after a while you feel insecure without it. A frame is essential if you want to explore more inventive techniques.

Traditional wooden embroidery frames for needlepoint are bulky contraptions, and it takes time to attach the canvas to them. For relatively small projects, we have used the wooden stretchers sold for mounting oil paintings. You can buy the pieces for these stretchers in art shops. They come in a variety of lengths so that you can make a frame of the size you require. The pieces are hammered together and the canvas can then be stretched over the frame and attached with drawing pins or staples. An old picture frame can be used instead.

We were delighted when we found what we consider to be the ideal frame. Like all good inventions it is based on a simple but very clever idea. It is made of plastic tubing and is easily assembled and dismantled. The canvas is clipped to the frame in a few minutes, and the arrangement is marvellous for travelling as the whole thing packs into a small

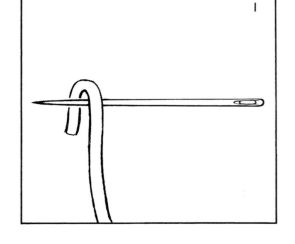

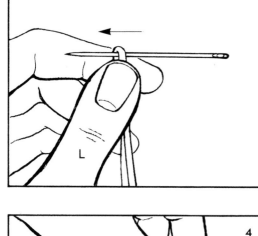

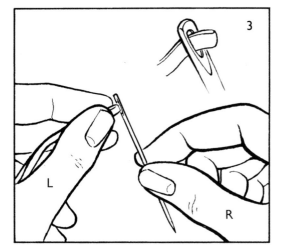

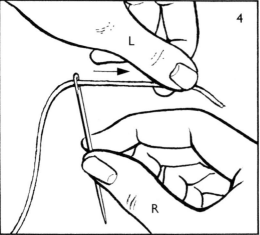

Fig. 4 *The best way to thread wool through a tapestry needle*

space and is very light. The tubes and connections are supplied in a variety of sizes, and you can mix and match them to make a frame of appropriate dimensions. They are available by mail order and the address of the manufacturer is given on p. 95.

HINTS TO HELP YOU

Cutting Canvas

You can cut canvas with almost any pair of scissors – kitchen scissors will do.

Because canvas is very strong, it could blunt small embroidery scissors, so it is best not to use these. Cut a piece large enough for your design, leaving at least 5 cm (2 in) of unworked canvas round the edges to enable the finished work to be stretched easily. Canvas edges are very scratchy; they will catch on your clothes and fray unless you turn them over or bind them. We used to make a 1 cm (½ in) turning and hand-sew it, using a running stitch occasionally anchored by a back stitch. Almost any sort of thread will do for this. Now we have adopted a much

24

quicker method: we simply bind the edges with masking tape.

If you are going to use a frame, the canvas must be big enough to fit comfortably over it. There should be a margin of about 3 cm (more than 1 in) all round your design, between it and the frame. If you extend the design too close to the edge of the frame you will find it difficult to stitch near the edges. As we have already explained, a reasonable margin is in any case necessary to give a good hold for stretching the finished canvas.

Selecting Threads

Preparing to sew is a bit like preparing to cook; you need a sufficient quantity of the basic ingredients, and it helps to get them out and check them before you begin the mixing. You can make up your own recipes and throw in a pinch of this and a dash of that to adjust the taste as you concoct your creation. So a collection of extra bits and bobs adds spice to what you produce.

You will need to spend time selecting the threads to work a new design, and this can be great fun. It may mean visiting a needlework shop to select wools, or simply searching through what you have already hoarded to find a suitable bouquet of shades. It is necessary to work hard on the decisions made at this stage. Leaving the colours in a pile so that you catch sight of them as you come into the room; rearranging them so that different colours are next to each other; and changing the proportion of certain

colours in the pile will help you to confirm or modify your choice. You can always change your mind as you stitch, but we find that it is not productive to begin until you are fairly confident of the basic plan.

Buying threads can be very expensive. To work a cushion will take about 75 g (3 oz) of wool. We have no inhibitions about using cheaper alternatives to tapestry wool when we can find them. Jumble sales, car-boot sales and charity shops occasionally yield rich harvests of embroidery materials, as well as knitting wools (often oddments) which are fine for our purposes. We look for pure wool of double-knitting thickness and enjoy incorporating multicoloured, tweedy, silky, sparkling and textured wools into our needlepoint. It takes time to build up a stock which will satisfy and stimulate your flights of fancy, and we squirrel away at collecting wools whenever the opportunity arises. If you have friends with a similar interest you can share your finds to increase your store.

Avoiding Tangles

This sounds simple, but surely we are not the only stitchers whose calm, creative rhythm has been broken by bouts of wrestling with hanks of wool which look like webs of confused spaghetti? You pull an end and it is always the wrong one, which only makes matters worse!

As threads are made into skeins by machine, those produced by one

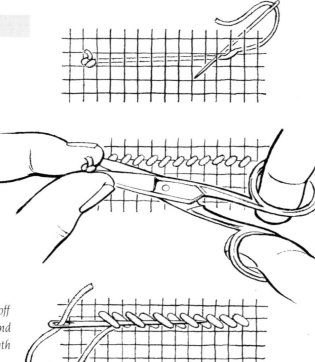

Fig. 5   *Starting off (top and centre) and finishing each length of thread*

Starting and Finishing

A piece of needlepoint will last a lifetime (or two, or more!) provided that the threads are firmly anchored so that they cannot come undone. We prefer to start with a knot on the top side of the work at a distance from the first stitch, which ensures that the thread is covered and held by subsequent stitches. The knot can be cut off once the thread is secured. This method prevents knots on the back causing a bumpy surface on the front of the work.

We finish simply by darning the end of the wool into adjoining stitches on the back of the work.

Choosing Stitches

The projects in this book can be worked in tent stitch or half-cross stitch (the latter uses less wool but does not cover the canvas quite as well or give quite such a regular tension).

There are, of course, many other canvas stitches, and thread manufacturers provide inexpensive dictionaries of them (see p. 95). You can have fun experimenting with new stitches to produce interesting effects.

manufacturer are always similarly wound, cut and labelled. There are two cut ends and one can be pulled smoothly while the other scrumples the hank into a knotted mess. Gentle experimentation with each make of wool will establish which end is which. When you have isolated the usable end, attach the other to the numbered label with a safety pin. This practice kills two birds with one stone. It means that you cannot pull the 'wrong' end because it is pinned, and it also stops the label slipping off the hank, thus ensuring that you know the make and shade in case you need to buy some more.

When you are stitching it is best not to use pieces of thread that are too long, or they will fray and twist as you sew. Approximately 45 cm (18 in) is a convenient length to use.

STORING SUPPLIES

Storage is easy at first. A plastic carrier bag holds your wools and a corner of the wardrobe hides a roll of canvas. However, if you become an embroidery addict, your collection of threads, canvas and frames will become increasingly bulky. In most homes storage space is at a premium and everyone and everything competes for what is available. The mark of a good storage system, like an efficiently programmed computer or a responsive brain, is that you can find what you want when you need it. It is infuriating to discover, when you have made do with inadequate materials, that you had the very thing you really needed tucked away tidily in a cupboard all the time.

We store canvas rolled up and tied with a label, on which we mark its gauge. We keep wool, silk and cotton threads in separate cardboard storage boxes. Within each box we sort them according to colour. Thus all red wools are kept together in a plastic freezer bag in the wool box. Freezer bags are useful for holding threads because you can easily see the contents. Frames can be dismantled for storage, and the pieces tied together and kept in a carrier bag. Small items like pins, needles and scissors can be kept in a cardboard drawer file.

Some people use their collection of threads for decoration, arranging wicker baskets or glass jars full of them on a shelf or windowsill or in an old fireplace. This can look beautiful but the reality of living with children, pets, dust, spills and splashes deters most stitchers from displaying threads in this way. When we are stitching we use wicker baskets to hold the materials, as these can be safely placed on the floor near where we are sitting and easily put away afterwards.

After a while you will probably accumulate books, paper, pencils, felt-tips, paints, glues, craft knives and other items useful for designing. You may manage to take over a corner of the house where you can keep all your materials and have space to work in. We have done this now that we have retired from full-time work. It is a luxury – by no means essential but wonderful if you can arrange it.

Fig. 6   Stitches for needlepoint

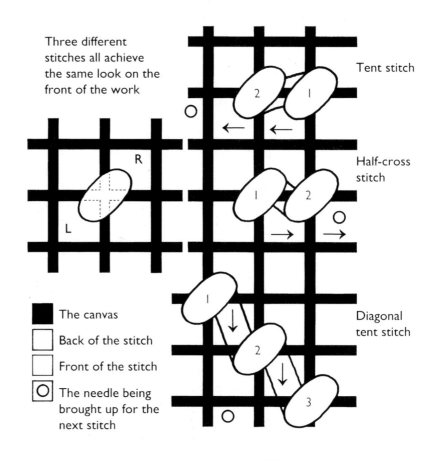

Three different stitches all achieve the same look on the front of the work

Tent stitch

Half-cross stitch

Diagonal tent stitch

■ The canvas

☐ Back of the stitch

☐ Front of the stitch

Ⓞ The needle being brought up for the next stitch

CUPBOARD LOVE

This project not only gives you a way of starting a design, it may also inspire you to tidy up a cupboard to make room for your materials! It is daunting to be faced with the task of filling an empty piece of canvas without a framework for your design or knowing where to begin. Try looking at a set of shelves, possibly inside a cupboard. You are going to make a picture of what you see. You do not have to choose anything complicated – shelves of books, rows of tins and packets, sets of mugs, piles of clothes or towels will do.

On a piece of canvas draw the outline of the top, bottom and sides of the cupboard or shelves and the divisions within them. Stitch these lines in the

Cupboard love. The wardrobe is not always as tidy as this! Note the stored canvas

appropriate colour. This will give you a framework, which you can fill in a piece at a time. The size of the framework will depend on the size of the picture you want to make, but it must be big enough for you to be able to work the shapes of the objects on the shelves. You may need to experiment with this.

At this point, try sorting the things on the shelves so that the arrangement pleases you. You may want to remove some items to make the picture simpler. Look at one shelf and draw the basic shapes of what you see onto the canvas. Choose colours from your collection of wools which

Bookshelves

correspond to the articles you have drawn, and fill in the shapes with stitches. Do not worry about embroidering detail; you can add this later if you want to.

Now complete the other shelves in the same way. Use artistic licence if you wish; this may be your only chance to change the hideous purple vase Aunt Ethel gave you into the beautiful blue one you always wanted! Finally, fill in the background.

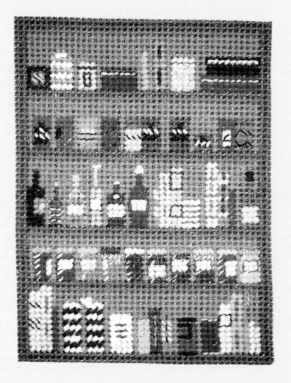

Kitchen store cupboard

29

CHAPTER 4

BENDING THE RULES

Crafts usually have rules which have evolved through the ages, being modified as new materials and techniques are discovered. Expertise is achieved by mastering the rules, and beginners can feel daunted by the need to do so. Artists, by contrast, often strive to break established rules.

Are there rules for needlepoint? If so, can they be broken? We would answer yes to both questions. Although you won't find rules neatly laid out in any book, there are certainly practices which are widely accepted and followed. Some are sensible basic principles if you want to produce durable and aesthetically pleasing work. We propose the following:

☐ Stitches should not come undone easily.
☐ Stitches should not unintentionally distort the background fabric.
☐ It should be possible to clean the work without spoiling it.
☐ The finished article should be fit for its intended purpose. (E.g. a cushion should be comfortable to lean on and reasonably hard-wearing. In comparison, a design intended to be hung on the wall may be uneven or delicate.)

We would suggest that other rules are really only conventions, and we enjoy challenging them. You can ignore them with impunity and still produce exciting

Variegated knitting wool was used to make the bricks for these houses

and functional work; in fact, following them slavishly will inhibit invention, exploration and experimentation.

WOOLS

It is often said that proper tapestry wools should always be used for needlepoint because of their durability and washability and the wide range of colours available. They are also dye-fast and the correct weight and thickness to cover canvas evenly. It may be that tapestry wools were once superior to other yarns in these respects, but we believe that most threads now meet the same

standards and can produce equally good results. Dry cleaning is, in any case, a reasonably cheap option if there are any doubts about washability. We have tried a number of alternatives to tapestry wool:

□ Knitting, darning and rug wool; cotton embroidery thread; silk and metallic threads; and even fine string. We are currently collecting plastic carrier bags in interesting colours to make a rug for the garden.
□ Mixing threads of differing types in the same stitch. For instance, fine silk

A variegated knitting wool and a variegated stranded cotton produce a dappled effect in a geometric design

31

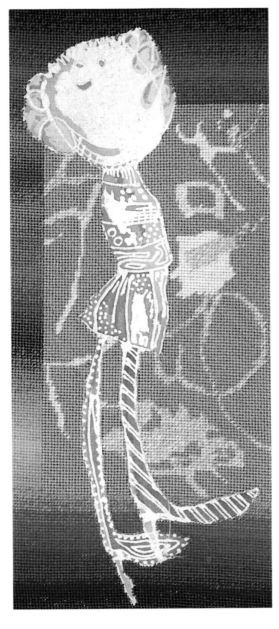

A five year old's drawing interpreted in batik and combined with a shaded background, worked on canvas with crewel wool

threaded alongside wool adds a flecked highlight to the stitch.

☐ Using different types of thread on different areas within the same piece of work. You soon get used to judging the thickness of threads and using several strands of the thinner ones so that an even effect is produced. Experimentation

will show what you need to cover the canvas to your satisfaction.

☐ Using crewel wool with two or more colours in the needle to create delicate shading. Crewel wool is about one-third the thickness of tapestry wool and is also used for sewing on very fine canvas, which can be covered by one or two strands.

☐ Working a small amount of fine thread on top of existing stitches. This can tone down a colour that does not look quite right, add texture, or define a feature that is too small for the fatter threads. We also use crewel wool, silk or sewing cotton to outline part of the design and to draw an emphasising line. The extra stitches are often sewn up and down the canvas squares rather than diagonally across them. The important thing is to produce the shape that you want.

TIDY BACKS

The majority of people who show interest in our work inspect the back as if it were as fascinating as the front. If it is reasonably ship-shape they mutter appreciatively. They seem to think that a tidy back is a sign of excellence. We wonder why. Where does this obsession come from? It is important that any knots or unevenness on the back should not distort the intended smoothness of the front, but in other respects the back of a piece of needlepoint is really unimportant. It is simply the place where you secure the threads.

Outlining in fine thread emphasises a shape that might otherwise be lost

That is not to say that the back is always uninteresting. It can be very pleasing to look at. Its randomly produced texture has a primitive, hand-made appearance. We have sometimes photographed part of the back of a piece because it was so interesting visually.

COVERING THE CANVAS

It is generally thought to be important to cover all the canvas with threads. If you have done canvas work before, you will know how the wool tends to twist and become thinner as you sew, leaving the canvas partly revealed because the wool has not covered it completely. You get the same effect if you use thread that is too thin for the canvas. This unintentional exposure of the canvas may detract from the design and can be avoided by using relatively short lengths of wool in the appropriate thickness.

There are, however, occasions when you may decide to bare the canvas as a deliberate ploy. You might paint or dye part of it and leave it exposed to give an interesting textural effect. Alternatively, you could let white canvas threads shine through your work to lighten it. Wool

This is the back of a design shown later in this book. Can you identify it?

colours are dense and it is often difficult to reproduce the lightness and brightness you are striving for.

STITCH DIRECTION

Needlepoint is usually worked in half-cross or tent stitch, with all the stitches sloping the same way. If you are covering large areas in one colour it is probably best to use tent stitch, working each stitch from bottom left to top right (or vice versa if you are left-handed) to give an even finish. You can turn the work round when you come to the end of a row so that you are always stitching in the same direction. Tent stitch covers the back of the canvas completely, as well as the front. Half-cross stitch is cheaper because it uses less thread but it is more difficult to keep smooth and even. It can give a slightly ridged effect if the tension is too great. When we are working a piece with a lot of different colours and shapes, we sometimes use a mixture of tent and half-cross stitch. This does not affect the appearance provided the half-cross stitch is not pulled too tight.

Needlepoint can look very odd if the stitches do not all slope in the same direction, but there are occasions when you might want to enhance your design by working stitches in different directions to create a particular effect. For instance, if the design includes lines travelling diagonally across the canvas, those going from bottom left to top right will look

different from those going from bottom right to top left. If it is essential to the design that both sets of lines should appear to be of equal width and smoothness, it will help if you stitch one set in the 'wrong' direction. Occasionally the design inspires you to paint on the canvas with stitches that vary both in length and direction. It is, of course, possible to stitch from any hole on the canvas to any other, but it is advisable to use a frame if you try this, as the tension is difficult to control otherwise.

The canvas for this design was painted with diluted oil-based paint and left to dry for a week before starting to stitch. It was important not to let any threads go across the back of the empty spaces in the pattern

Bird cushion. This was worked in crewel wool, enabling up to three colours to be used in each stitch

TINY STITCHES

People often seem to think that the finer the canvas the more impressive the piece. It certainly impresses us to see people doing very fine work. You know it will take ages to complete! Yet it is possible to create exquisite and subtle work on canvas of medium or large mesh, and we generally prefer to work quickly and to produce the desired effect with as little

pain as possible. Thus we do not usually stitch very fine canvas, although there are times when it is appropriate.

We knew a teenager who supplemented her pocket money by making tapestry rugs for doll's houses. It did not help her eyesight much, but she worked tiny motifs in detail by using extremely fine canvas and one strand of crewel wool. The results were beautiful miniatures,

36

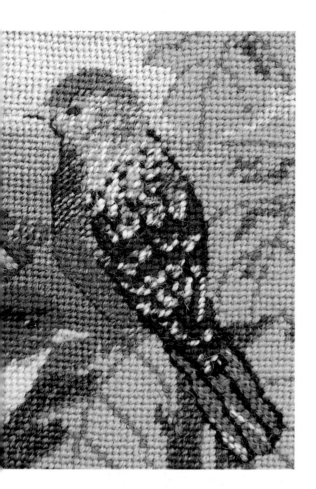

perfectly to scale. At the other extreme, if you stitch a rug on very coarse canvas with thick wool, you will have trouble keeping it rectangular. The finished article will be large and heavy, and difficult to stretch back into shape. Coarse canvas distorts more easily than fine canvas, and working it may not demonstrate your needle skill to its best advantage. Nevertheless, you may still be able to produce results with charm and panache.

MIXED MEDIA

It is rare to find mixed-media embroidery incorporating needlepoint, probably because it is relatively bulky and heavy. We have thoroughly enjoyed mixing our work with other crafts. Combinations we have tried include:

☐ Needlepoint applied onto a knitted background. It is much quicker to cover

Left: Ornithologists will recognise the rare woolly finch, whose shape is captured by stitches going in the 'wrong' direction

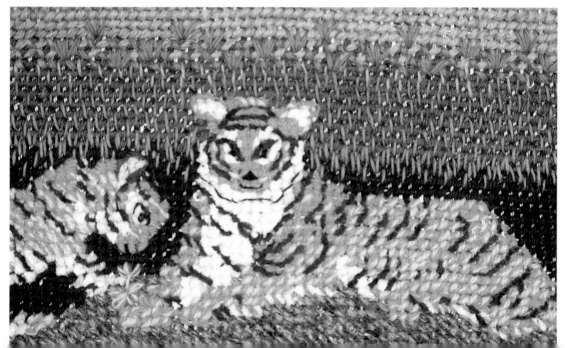

Tiger worked in oddments of chunky knitting wool on rug canvas, proving you don't have to work on a small scale to produce intricate effects!

This knitted landscape was backed with strong cotton fabric so that the animals and the ark (which is worked on canvas) could be sewn onto it. The tortoises are worked on canvas too

a large area with wool by knitting rather than sewing it, and knitting can make interestingly coloured or textured backgrounds.

- A batik picture on cotton stitched onto the canvas before the background was worked in half-cross stitch.
- Small mirrors attached to textured canvas work in a single colour. This was inspired by a piece of shisha mirror embroidery from India.
- Photographs and small pictures incorporated into needlepoint, or a needlepoint picture mounted next to the photograph from which it was derived.

USES FOR NEEDLEPOINT

Some books seem to suggest that you can make a wide variety of things out of needlepoint, but we have found that its uses are limited. Because it is strong,

38

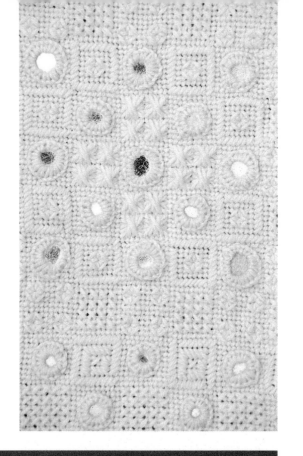

fairly stiff and heavy, it is good for making cushions, covering chair seats, stools or kneelers, and making carpets, pictures or large bags. Everything else we have attempted looks out of scale and would have been better made in another type of embroidery. Needlepoint is not suitable for making items in which the hang of the fabric is important, or where softness and pliability are required. In this book we have therefore confined ourselves to projects suitable for cushions, pictures, large bags or rugs.

Shisha mirrors are usually incorporated into multicoloured silk embroideries. Here they are used with a neutral shade of wool worked in textured stitches

Capturing the light on the sea was a challenge, solved by using knitting yarn with a metallic sheen

39

PROJECT FOUR

THE LOWRY EFFECT

The purpose of this project is to experiment with shapes, using stitches going in different directions. The design will consist of a lot of small figures, as in a painting by L. S. Lowry. The figures must be as active as possible. You could make a cushion or a picture for someone keen on jogging, aerobics, golf, gardening or swimming. You could show children playing, a lot of people on a beach or on a railway platform, or people climbing or shopping. Make the figures small; we suggest the head should be two stitches square. Make them look as though they are moving. It is fun to dress them and to experiment with hairstyles and details, but you may prefer to try silhouettes in one colour. The background could be a single colour or shaded in some way, but it should be fairly simple to show the figures to best effect.

First try drawing stick-figures by colouring in the tiny squares on graph paper (see fig. 7). When you have produced some you like, try stitching them on canvas, working the majority of stitches in the conventional direction but stitching arms, legs, etc. in the direction necessary to give the movement and thickness you want. The more you experiment the easier it will become.

When the figures are done, fill in the background, again working the majority of stitches in the conventional direction but inserting a stitch going the 'wrong' way when you want to emphasise an existing shape. Add fine detail or small stitches to improve the outline of a figure after you have worked the background. If you are not sure where to place the figures, you could divide the canvas into squares and

Fig. 7   *It helps to draw the figures on a scrap of graph paper*

40

put a person in each one, or make rows of figures across the canvas. If you want to place them randomly you may find it easiest to make a rough plan of stick-figures on a piece of graph paper.

We hope you enjoy playing with this idea and inventing lots of variations on the simple theme.

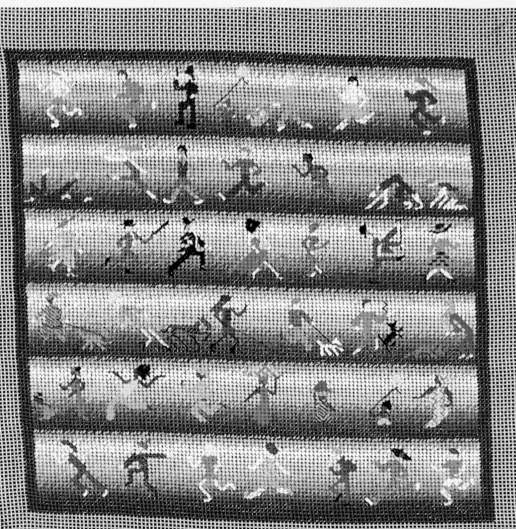

Above: *The basic figure has a head two stitches square, a body six stitches by two, and legs six stitches long. A single stitch is used for the neck, and the arms are usually five stitches long*

The Lowry Effect. The figures are set in motion using stitches worked in different directions

CHAPTER 5

PLAYING WITH PAPER

Time spent playing with a new idea is never wasted. Stitching is a slow method of producing an effect, and you want to be fairly confident that a design will work before you begin the laborious process of embroidering it. Playing with paper is a relatively quick and inexpensive way of experimenting and trying out a lot of ideas. If you do not like the results you can throw them away without feeling that you have wasted a lot of energy. This sort of experimentation allows you to create images for part or all of a design, to discover new colour relationships and, most important of all, to practise composition.

Some people have a natural eye for composition and can put things together to make a pleasing design without any effort. Most of us have to work hard to achieve a visual balance of shape, line and texture. Yet, however skilled we are, we can all learn from practice and from thinking carefully about composition.

In this chapter we suggest ways of composing images using coloured paper, cuttings from magazines and newspapers, wallpaper remnants, card from packaging, or scraps of fabric.

Opposite: This design was created by tearing holes in three different wrapping papers, which were then placed one on top of the other. (Folding the paper first makes it easier to tear the shapes out of the middle)

CUTTING

- ☐ Try 'drawing' by cutting – it is easier than it sounds. Take a piece of paper (scrap paper will do) and choose an object to 'draw'. Use scissors to cut out the shape of the object. Do not draw it in pencil first, just look at it carefully and start cutting. Try as many times as you need to get a satisfying image of the object. You could make a collection of these shapes and stick them on paper to create a design. If you feel confident enough, try making cut-out shapes of your family (faces or whole bodies) and arranging these so that they form an interesting group before sticking them down. You will probably want to overlap them.

- ☐ Children love cutting folded paper and opening it up to see the design they have made. You could experiment by folding paper in different ways to produce different patterns. Remember to leave part of each fold uncut; if you do not, the pattern will fall apart when you unfold it. Try cutting patterns out of three different sorts of paper (e.g. newspaper, wrapping paper and a magazine picture) and placing these on top of one another so that one shows through the holes in another. Move them around and stick them down when you have made an arrangement that satisfies you.

- ☐ Choose a full-page colour image from a magazine and cut it roughly across from side to side in strips of different sizes. Remake the picture on a sheet of coloured paper, then play with the strips, moving them so that they are no longer in line, until you get a pleasingly distorted image.

- ☐ You can distort a linear pattern or drawing by cutting it into strips and then separating them before sticking

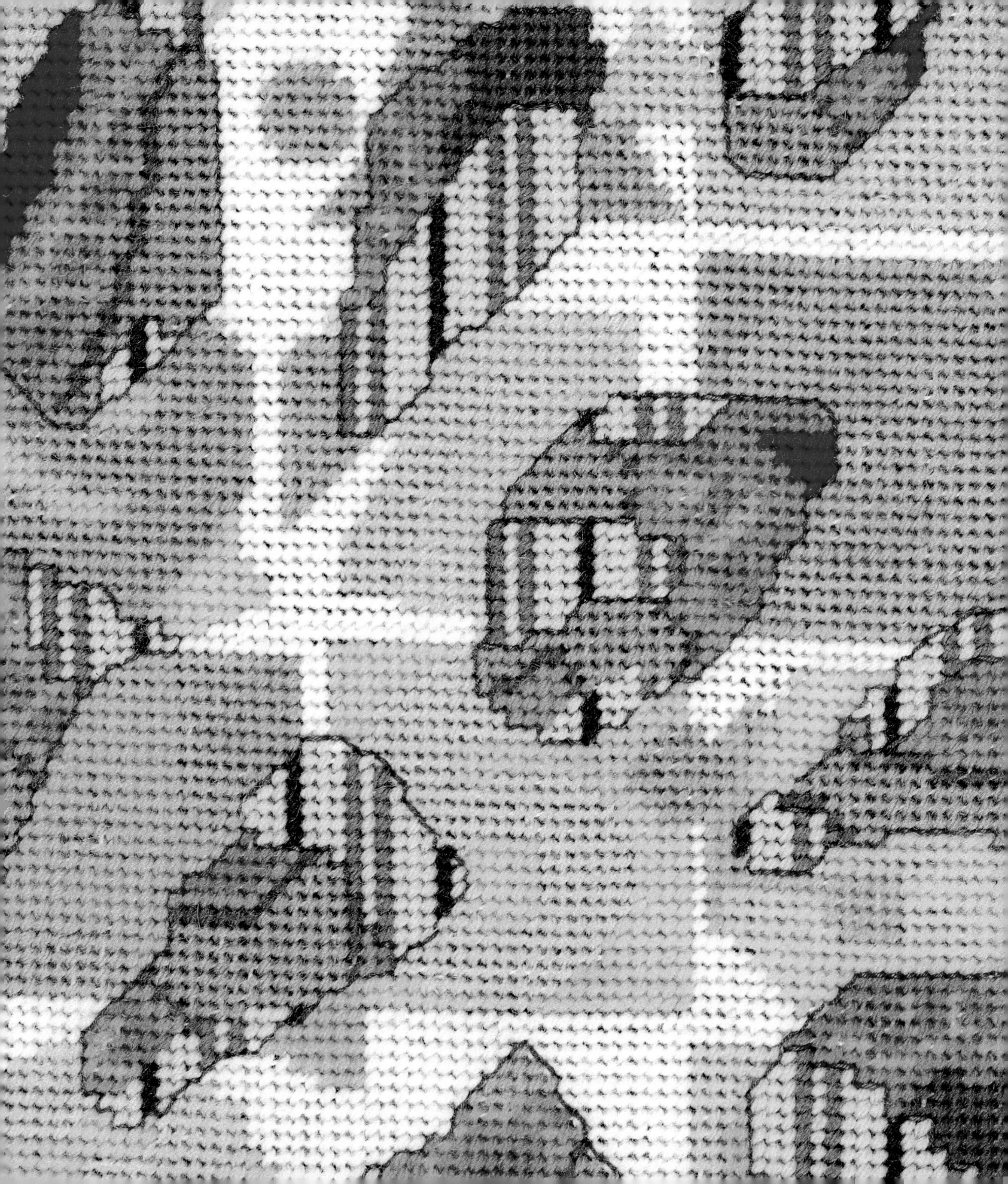

For this design, shapes were drawn to resemble strips of torn paper and three different patterns stitched in them

them onto another sheet. Try adding lines to connect the shapes in the strips.

You might find the results of your cutting and sticking would make an interesting piece of needlepoint. Even if you do not like the whole effect, you can use a spy-hole, as suggested in Project 8 (p. 82), to find an area that interests you. Alternatively, tear an unsuccessful attempt into pieces and rearrange them to see whether you can make a more satisfying image.

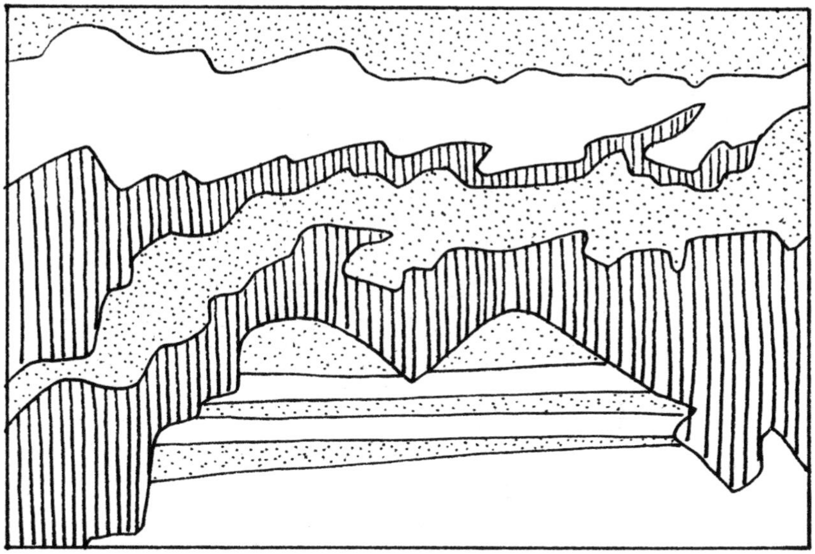

TAKING RUBBINGS

As a child you probably made rubbings of coins by placing them under a piece of paper and scribbling over the top with a pencil. Try exploring the same technique to make images of textures which could be stitched as part of a design. Use lining paper and a wax crayon to make impressions of tree bark, the backs of leaves, embossed flooring, brickwork, cracked stone or paving, and manhole covers. Again, you can cut and stick the results to make more interesting patterns if you wish.

STENCILLING

Take the front from a cereal packet and cut an interesting but simple shape out of the middle to make a stencil. Place it over a sheet of paper and colour the exposed shape with paint or crayon. Move the stencil and fill the shape with another colour. If you overlap the shapes you will get a third colour. Dab the paint on with a piece of crumpled kitchen paper to give a textured effect, or spray it on if you wish. A cardboard shape could be used to mask part of the background – dab or spray

Figs. 8 and 9
Abstract design (above)
based on rubbings from
paving stones (below)

45

Stencilling techniques

round it to leave its uncoloured image on the paper. To add straight lines to your design, use masking tape before applying the paint.

MAKING COLLAGES

You can have great fun making pictures by cutting out images, rearranging them and sticking them on a background. The pictures may be representational or abstract. First try tearing shapes out of different sorts of paper. Newsprint looks striking intermingled with coloured paper. A piece of wallpaper can make an interesting background and you can sometimes beg old books of wallpaper samples from DIY shops. You can, of course, use fabric as well as paper to make collages.

COMPOSING

Remember the purpose of all this activity is to help you think about composition: the relationship between the shapes, and the spaces between them. It is worth keeping your more successful efforts and displaying them for a while so that you can continue to look at them.

Playing with paper also enables you to experiment with colour. When you design work on canvas it is very easy to get into a rut, using similar colour combinations all the time. To break out of this, try searching through magazines or fabrics and making two piles. One should contain the colours you love, the other those you loathe. Make a collage from each pile. Then cut the collages into pieces and make a new arrangement

46

using at least one-third of the loathsome colours mixed with the others.

Another way of kicking over the traces, if you can afford it, is to go to an embroidery shop and make a selection of new threads, choosing only colours you hate. You might be surprised, when you look at them in a bunch, by how interesting they are together and be inspired to try them in a design. (If, on the other hand, you still dislike them heartily you can always put them back on the rack and go home with your bank balance unscathed!)

DRAWING

We hope to show, throughout this book, that you do not have to be able to draw or paint to design for needlepoint. However, if you do enjoy drawing it is obviously a tremendous help. We are both still trying to learn and have been to classes, some more useful than others. What we have been taught about line, tone, proportion and composition has affected our designs and made us willing to have a go at drawing what we would previously have copied. Deciding to go to classes is a bit like joining Weight Watchers. You are committed to attempting to improve. We found that being made to draw quickly and to share our efforts with the rest of the class really helped. Drawing with a thick white crayon or painting with a sponge rather than a brush led us to stop worrying about our inadequacies and, in consequence, to produce work that pleased us. We will carry on trying. You could have a go too.

Collages showing experiments with colour. Don't forget that food can be a good source for design!

PROJECT FIVE

BALANCING ACT

After a brightly coloured polyanthus pattern had been stitched, a much lighter version was attempted, not very successfully. Woollen stitches produce such dense blocks of colour that you have to use extremely pale tones to achieve a light effect

This is a project to help you experiment with a lot of colours and to think about composition as you gradually build up an arrangement of simple shapes.

Make a design composed of small squares or triangles (see fig. 10). Start in the middle of the canvas with your first square. Each time you add an adjacent square, use different colours and think about what they look like together. As the design grows, decide where you want to have particularly dark or light areas, and keep looking at the balance of colour.

If you do not want to use a geometric shape for your pattern, choose a more organic one, e.g. a flower head or plant cell. Such shapes may not fit together exactly and you may have to fill in the background, but try to place them as close as possible so that you can see the effect of putting different colours next to one another.

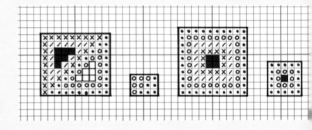

Fig. 10

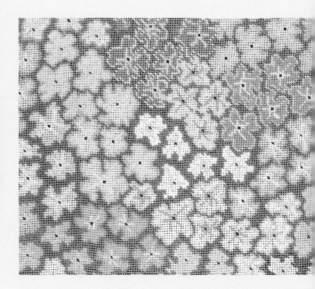

Balancing Act. This
cushion used almost
every colour in our wool
collection

CHAPTER 6

FINDING HELP

So here you are with a brain bursting with stored images, and a cupboard overflowing with materials. How do you begin a piece of needlepoint? You need to know where to start.

The process of designing involves lots of choices and decisions. It is partly a matter of elimination, of discarding unattractive options until you are sure what it is you want to do. Some decisions are relatively easy. For instance, if you have a new chair and want to make a cushion for it, you already know approximately what size it should be. You may also want to use colours that match the chair or the room. Even if you have no precise idea about colours, you will find that, when you think about it, you quickly eliminate a lot that you would not find pleasing in this context, leaving you to choose from a relatively limited range. You probably also have a feeling about whether a simple or complex design would look best. So your choices are already narrowed down, but many still remain to be made before you can begin sewing, and others will have to be made as the work proceeds.

SHARING DECISIONS

One of the easiest ways to begin is to get somebody else to make some decisions for you by accepting a commission from family or friends. Talk to them to find out precisely what they want. For example, a brother has bought two small bedroom chairs and wants new seats for them. He would like the two designs to be different but related. The background should tone with the carpet, which is cocoa-coloured. He lives in an old farmhouse and it would be nice if the designs reflected this. How about using farm animals? This seems daunting, but don't panic! Plenty of help is available. You can use someone else's work as a basis for your own. This isn't as reprehensible as it sounds; in fact, it is the beginning of most new designs. People do not design in a vacuum – they are constantly influenced by their surroundings. If you don't think you can draw the animals yourself, look around to see what pictures you can find.

The pictures that inspired us in this particular instance were very easy to adapt because they were already used in needlepoint. *Noah's Ark*, a book of needlepoint designs collected by Hugh Ehrman and Elizabeth Benn (see p. 95), contains a picture of sheep in misty Welsh pastures by Sarah Windrum and a splendid cow called Pansy, designed by Kaffe Fassett. The problem was no longer how to stitch the animals, therefore. It was how to incorporate their very different sizes and shapes into two designs that would look good together. The solution was to enclose them both in similar circles of green grass. The sheep were surrounded by a wreath of daisies traced from a flower book, and the cow was ringed with buttercups similarly reproduced. The sheep were moved around a bit to fit into the circle, and an

Opposite: *This lamb was added to fill a space in the chair seat design*

extra lamb was added to fill up a space. The cow was changed from its original Friesian black to some unknown breed of chestnut brown. The background was to be cocoa-coloured, but it looked a bit flat and boring against the lovely brown cow. *How Now?* seemed an appropriate inscription for her, and working these words repeatedly in a lighter shade gave the background a mottled effect. (All rather silly and not obvious unless you peer at the chair closely, but it made the whole thing much more fun to do. The sheep are munching grass against a faint pattern exhorting them to *Safely Graze.*)

COPYRIGHT

The work shown on pp. 51–2 is an adaptation of designs by Kaffe Fassett and Sarah Windrum, who – together with the publisher of the book *Noah's Ark* – kindly gave us permission to reproduce it here. Nevertheless, the piece was worked by Ann strictly for her own use. If it had been sold, even on the smallest craft stall, she would have been in breach of copyright, as she has used someone else's designs. You need to be aware, therefore, of the laws of copyright whenever you borrow ideas from other sources.

Designs adapted from Kaffe Fassett's 'Pansy the cow' and Sarah Windrum's 'Sheep at Cwmcarvan'

DEVELOPING THEMES

Kaffe Fassett was unwittingly responsible for another gift. In his book *Glorious Needlepoint* (see p. 95) is a chapter called 'Faces', containing a pattern for a cushion based on a Kabuki face with wonderful liquid eyes. Eyes are hard enough to draw but even more difficult to sew; these ones were fascinating and inspired experimentation. Making the rest of the face equally realistic would have been very difficult, but the book also included a clown's face, which was sufficiently stylised for those with scant drawing skills to produce a reasonable result. The design was quickly worked into a clown cushion for a six-year-old boy. He was very pleased with it, and his three-year-old sister admired it, too, and wanted a similar gift.

As often happens, working on this design suggested other possibilities. You can understand why artists go through periods of exploring a theme. As you sit sewing and thinking about what you are doing, new ideas grow. Your first efforts at a subject suggest better and different ways of approaching it. So a clown picture for the three year old was an attractive proposition. A library book about clowning and the traditional patterns used by famous circus artists provided lots of shapes to choose from. The canvas was divided into boxes of bright colour with a clown's face in each. The shape of the first face was chosen by cutting paper heads to fit in the box until one that looked right was found. When this was done, the

others were all made to the same size. Decisions had to be made about whether to make the face look happy or sad, and which make-up to apply, but this was enjoyable and relatively easy once the basic arrangement had been fixed. Unfortunately, our second attempt was not received as enthusiastically as the first. The little girl thanked us politely, but the picture did not stay on her bedroom wall for long. She complained that she could not sleep with all those nasty men in the room!

This clown cushion was worked in the knitting wools that were to hand when a bout of flu made shopping impossible

The scary clowns

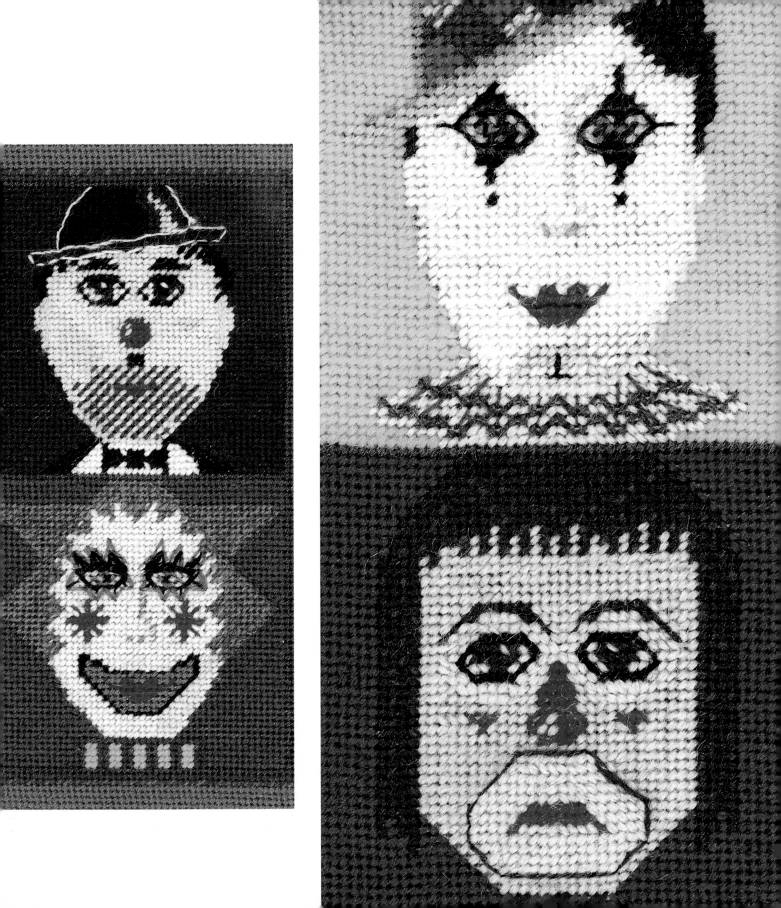

TWO PROJECTS

The examples already described in this chapter show some of the ways in which we have made decisions about designs, but they do not include full details of the working methods. It might be helpful now to consider exactly how we each tackled a project of our own, which at first seemed too difficult. We had to devise ways of overcoming the difficulties, and although we were pleased with the results we had to struggle (and seek assistance) to achieve them.

ROSES

Ann: I have always liked embroideries featuring roses, and admired professional designs for their shading and three-dimensional effect. A new duvet cover with a yellow and pink rose pattern prompted me to have a go at a rose design of my own. First, however, I had to find answers to a lot of questions. The creative process was something like this:

Q   What do I want to make?
A   A rose-patterned cushion to go on the green chair in the bedroom.
Q   What colours shall I use?
A   Pinks and yellows to match the duvet material. I will need several shades of each colour – I think five is the most I could manage. I will also need several shades of green for the leaves.
Q   What sort of background would look good?

A   I want to make the roses stand out and to concentrate on working them. The chair is quite a dark green, so I think a plain, light-green background would be suitable and would certainly contrast with the pinks and yellows.
Q   Where shall I find the roses?
A   It's November and there are only tattered buds in the garden. I do have some photographs of roses but none of them is quite what I want – they look too flat. I try some growers' catalogues and find two differently shaped roses of a suitable size. (One is red rather than pink but I hope I will be forgiven for changing the colour and creating a new variety.) I decide to use them.
Q   How shall I arrange the roses on the cushion? There are lots of possibilities (see fig. 11).
A   I decide on a garland. I draw a circle on the canvas using a dinner plate and an HB pencil. (A softer pencil shows up better but tends to come off on the wool and make it look dirty.) The roses will be arranged round this circle. I like the size of the roses in the photograph; they are big enough to allow me to experiment with shading, and small enough to fit round the wreath. I think six will be enough, and decide to arrange them symmetrically round the circle and afterwards to fill in the spaces with buds and leaves.
Q   How shall I translate the rose photographs into patterns for needlepoint?

A   This is the most difficult bit for me and I have to try several times until I get something that looks reasonable. I have just discovered graph tracing paper. You can buy it in a number of grid sizes corresponding to different gauges of canvas. I am using ten squares to 2.5 cm (1 in). I trace the general shape of each rose first, then place a fresh piece of tracing paper over the traced outline and try to shade it, using different symbols for each of my five wools (see figs 12 and 13). This involves studying the photographs to decide where the light and shadows fall.

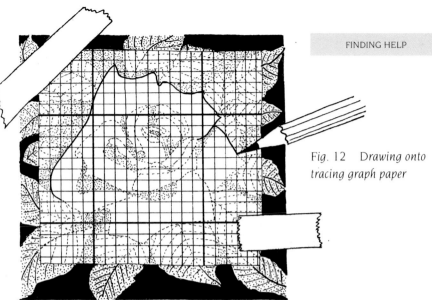

Fig. 12   *Drawing onto tracing graph paper*

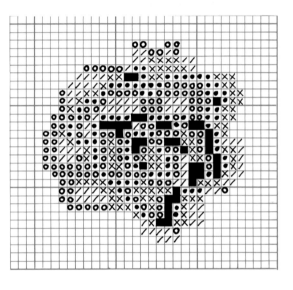

Fig. 13   *Placing symbols on a tracing. The symbols represent the five tones to be used, ranging from light to dark, as follows:*

○ / ✗ ● ■

Q   Where shall I begin to embroider?
A   I decide to try a yellow rose to see whether the shading works. I begin approximately in the middle of the rose, placing it on the circle at the top of the wreath. I try several times, working from my graph-paper chart and adjusting the shading each time until I feel I've done my best. I then try a pink rose placed one-sixth of the way round the circle, and make several attempts before I am

Left: Fig. 11   *Rough sketches showing possible ways of arranging the roses*

satisfied with it. I work the other roses in the same manner, each one-sixth of the way round the circle.

Q   The roses still look two-dimensional and do not have the depth I wanted. How can I make them look more rounded?

A   I decide to outline the petal shapes in order to emphasise them. I want to draw fine lines but I do not have any fine wool of the right colour. I decide to use sewing cotton. Again I have to experiment several times until I feel I've got the stitching right. I am pleased with the effect. When I screw up my eyes and peer at the roses from a distance they even seem to bear some relationship to the originals!

Q   How shall I complete the garland?

A   I need to draw the whole pattern. I draw the circle and the rough outlines of the roses on the graph tracing paper. I trace some buds from the catalogue photographs, shade them as well as I can and place them near the roses. I make several attempts at drawing leaf shapes to fill in the rest of the garland, until I have an arrangement I like.

Q   How shall I shade the leaves?

A   I decide this does not matter very much. I have four shades of green and decide to use two or three on each leaf to emphasise its shape. I use the darkest to make veins and stalks. I then work the rest of the wreath from the graph-paper chart.

Q   What next?

A   I'm afraid all that remains is a lot of boring pale-green background. (In fact, I did some of this as I went along, when I was tired of trying to follow the chart and deciding how to colour the leaves.)

The final result looks good on the chair by the bed and is quite different from anything I have done before. The process described above could be used for translating all kinds of photographs or drawings into needlepoint. An alternative method is to buy a transparent plastic grid, place it over the picture and work directly onto the canvas, square by square.

Fig. 14   The final drawing for the Roses design shown opposite

Right: *Ann's Roses*

58

SEASIDE BIRDS

Jennie: It is often difficult to say where ideas come from – the important thing is that they come! On one occasion, however, I knew exactly what the source of my inspiration was. I spent an autumn weekend near a shingle beach and found it visually fascinating. I was particularly excited by the birds, the incredible variety of stones and shells among the shingle, and the rather cold northern light. (You may think me easily excited, but I'm an urban dweller, after all!) I wanted to make something which captured all this. I took a lot of photographs but no single one held all that I had enjoyed so much.

Before I discuss how I arrived at my design, I want to consider an interesting aspect of problem-solving. Have you ever gone to sleep with a problem that seemed overwhelming and woken in the morning to find that the solution was obvious? It is as if your brain has put everything in order, discarded unworkable ideas and come up with the answer without any help from you. I find that the process of designing is partly subconscious. Looking, looking again and thinking about an idea gives you a lot of possibilities to consider. When you come to make conscious decisions you often find that your brain has continued to work on the ideas without your knowledge, and the choices are easier than they seemed before. This process is difficult to describe because it is largely intuitive. I have tried below to record the conscious elements of my seaside design and to reconstruct those parts which must have been subconscious.

Action Put some of the seaside photographs up on the wall.

Thought What a huge space I was looking at. How could that sense of space be worked on canvas? The sparkle on the sea: would glittering threads capture it? The sea disappearing into the sky. What must it be like to soar like a bird? How could I show the power of wings? How alert birds look at rest: their bodies might be still but their eyes are restless and bright. The smoothness of the large pebbles nearest the shoreline …

Action Washed and dried shell collection.

Thought How could I include shells and suggest their curves and spirals in such a vast space? None of them could be seen in my photographs except where I had taken close-ups.

Fig. 15 The first idea for Seaside Birds (p. 63)

60

Brainwave I woke the next day with a solution. Border the large space with a shell design. Make it a cushion – a border would look odd in a picture.

Thought Problem – a border would leave even less room on the canvas to create a sense of distance and space.

Brainwave Work a soaring bird in front of the border, i.e. overlapping it. This would make the bird look higher off the ground.

Action Visited library for pictures of sea-birds. Looked through old cross-stitch patterns for birds. (Cross-stitch shapes work equally well on canvas. Knitting charts are less easy to translate because each stitch represents a rectangle rather than a square.)

Thought Did it matter if the birds were the actual species I saw? Not really, but there must be gulls. After looking at some pictures, I had a rough idea of what I wanted to do.

Action Very small sketch, just placing things (see fig. 18).

Thought I needed something to join up the shells otherwise they looked too separate. Seaweed was a possibility.

Action I traced those birds that corresponded with my initial idea.

Thought They were far too small (about 2.5 cm/1 in high). I could only trace the major lines. How would I know what size to make them?

Brainwave Draw the rough design to scale on graph paper.

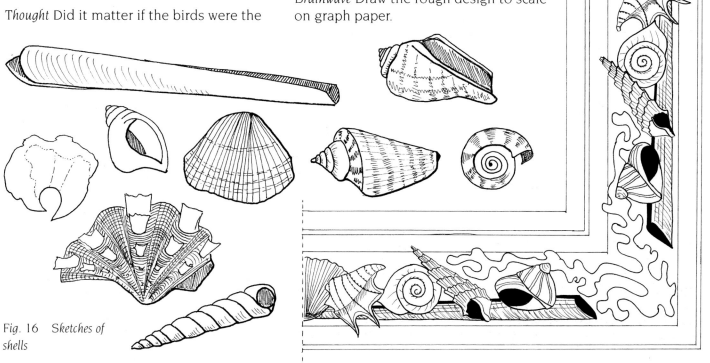

Fig. 16   *Sketches of shells*

Fig. 17   *The first idea for the border*

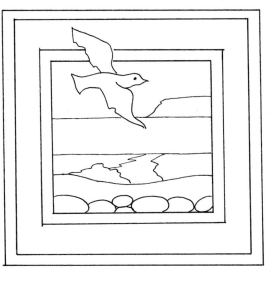

Fig. 18 *This rough sketch of the final design helped in deciding where to place some more sea-birds*

Action Decided size.

Thought Border would have to be quite big if shells were to have enough detail. I needed to simplify the design – this would also help to create the illusion of space (see fig. 19).

Fig. 19 *The simplified version of the border*

Action Drew rough design to scale on graph paper.

Thought I had to draw only a section of the border; this could be rotated and repeated all the way round (see fig. 20).

Action Visited photocopy shop. Enlarged traced birds to 400%. Cut them out and tried positioning them on the rough design. Finalised sketch (see fig. 21).

Thought I still needed only the major lines because I could experiment with detail as I stitched.

Action Transferred design onto canvas.

Brainwave Colours – blues, browns/rusts. (This idea was probably inspired by the fabric covering my new sofa, but it also seemed appropriate for the theme.) I would need stone, beige and grey as well as richer browns.

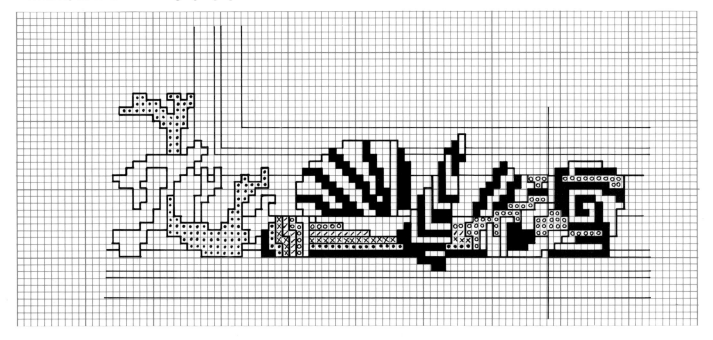

Jennie's Seaside Birds

63

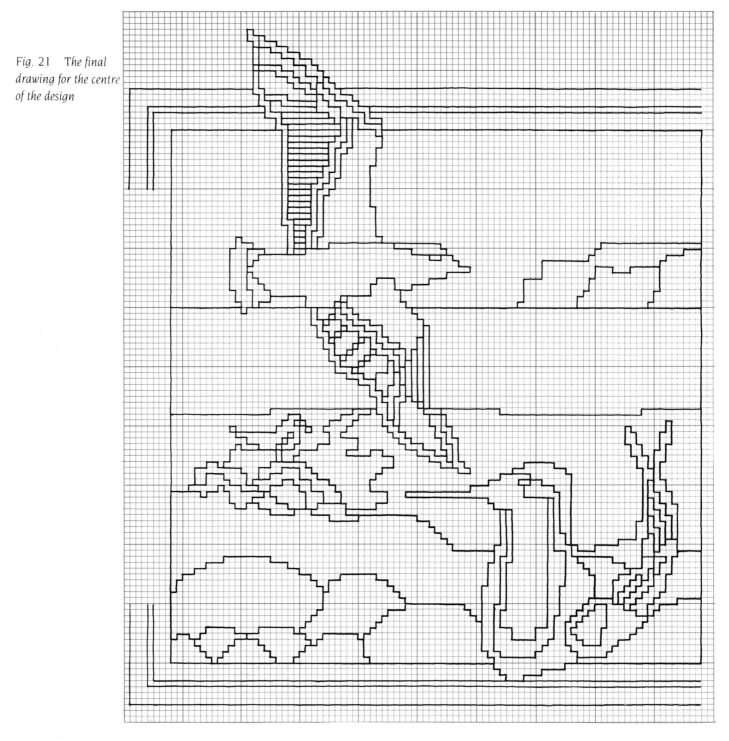

Fig. 21   The final
drawing for the centre
of the design

Action Collected wools. Started stitching large pebbles.

Thought I was not sure if I could make the pebbles look smooth enough using canvas of ten holes to 2.5 cm (1 in). The large pebbles did, however, look surprisingly smooth. The small ones had to be darker to show off the large ones. I tried three colours but I could not make them look like pebbles and went to bed in disgust.

Brainwave Alternate colours give a scrunchy, textured look. Much better and very simple.

Action Embroidered outline of large sitting gull.

Thought I was doing this first because I was a bit nervous of working the glittery sea.

Brainwave I could pattern the sea, making it gradually paler as it melted into the sky.

Action Tried this. It looked good. Finished the sea. Came back to do birds, using library-book pictures to add detail to the shapes. I worked straight onto the canvas without drawing the detail first.

The finished result was quite a breakthrough for me. I had previously been experimenting with more abstract designs.

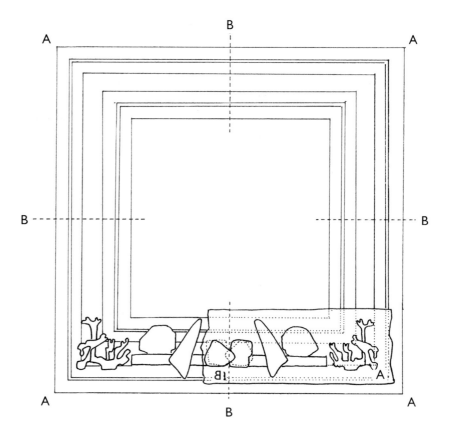

SOME USEFUL TIPS

□ The best results are achieved by using the best sources. If you start by tracing a sentimentalised or poorly drawn image, that is what you will reproduce.
□ Children's books often have good, simple illustrations. Do not forget to look at them when you are raiding your local library.
□ Once you have got the basic shapes right you can make the image your own by adding detail.
□ You can turn tracing paper over to get a mirror image of the original shape, if desired.

Fig. 20 The border was repeated in sections around the central design

Left: *Cross-stitch design worked on canvas in tent stitch*

Above: *The same shape reversed (i.e. taken first from one and then from the other side of the tracing paper) and worked in different colours*

□ Photocopying is a very useful way of enlarging and reducing images. It can be expensive but is quick and easy. If you have a drawing programme on a personal computer, experiment by drawing the shapes you want. You can then very simply enlarge, reduce, rotate or duplicate the required shapes.

□ It may be possible to adapt an existing needlepoint design. Cross-stitch patterns are equally good.

□ You can also borrow techniques from other people, cultures and crafts. This may be highly experimental and may not prove useful in the end, but by trying new ideas, you improve your technical skills and define the limitations of the medium. You really don't know where the boundaries are until you explore them.

This was an experiment; the canvas was batiked and then stitched

PROJECT SIX

ANIMAL ANTICS

*Right: This large
picture was stitched on
rug canvas using rug
wool and thick knitting
wool. The giraffe and
some of the foliage were
worked with strips of
fabric (see also p. 37)*

Here is an idea to help you try out some
of the techniques we have described in
this chapter and to combine different
pictures of interestingly shaped and
patterned animals. Imagine that your
nephew, who is four, has asked you to
make a wild animal picture for his wall.

He has recently visited the zoo for the
first time and was thrilled to see some of
the animals he has always loved in
storybooks. He says he wants the picture
to be 'like a zoo but without cages'. He
does not mind how many animals there
are but he likes those with patterns on
their skin. He also likes monkeys 'because
they are naughty'! Choose any size of
canvas you like and make a small or large
picture.

*In contrast to the flights
of fancy in the previous
design, the animals are
here shown in their
natural habitat.
Monkeys would not be
happy here!*

CHAPTER 7

CREATING PATTERNS

Many images that survive from ancient primitive societies contain very simple shapes strung together in a pattern. Marks made on stone or wood, or on the earth itself, were often systematically repeated. Again, we are reminded of the computer analogy. Like a computer the human brain can reproduce an action many times in an organised way (but, unlike a computer, seems to gain satisfaction from the process).

Patterns are often passed down from generation to generation and become important cultural symbols. If you look at bark paintings, totem poles or sand patterns you can see examples of patterning that have become part of a culture's heritage. From an early age, children can produce lively repetitive patterns without the help of adults. The marks they make on paper, in a sandpit or on the beach seem to be a way of developing manipulative skills and laying down pathways within the brain.

REPEATING SHAPES

Many patterns are symmetrical but they do not have to be so. They are usually the result of repeating simple shapes, but they can produce complex as well as simple images. Patchworkers and quilters have always used them, and their traditional designs, such as Schoolhouse, Evening Star and Log Cabin, can easily be adapted for stitching on canvas. This type of pattern is a good starting point for people who are not used to creating their own designs. The joy of such work is that you can concentrate on choosing colours because, once the basic design has been

Right: *Patchwork patterns: Heavenly Steps, Schoolhouse, Evening Star and Log Cabin*

Far right: *This pattern looks quite complex but is composed of very simple elements*

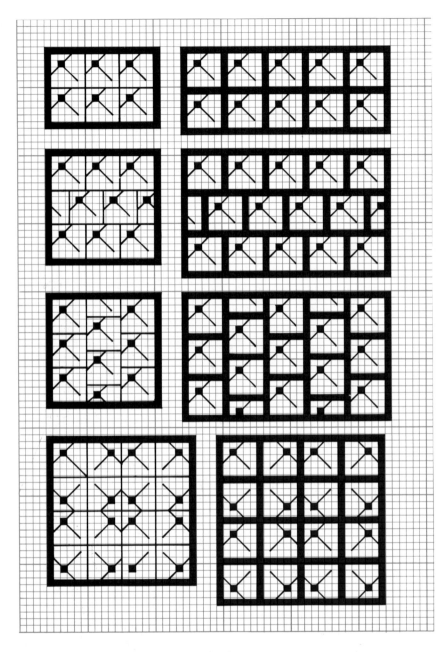

because you have made a mistake! Mistakes are usually difficult to hide in precise designs because they distort the pattern.) Incidentally, this type of design is rarely found in printed kits because it is difficult to print accurately on canvas.

It is possible to multiply a single shape in many different ways, e.g. some methods of repeating a square pattern are shown in fig. 22. Repeats can be joined to cover the space completely or separated so that a background shows through.

DIVIDING STRIPES

Another simple way of producing an interesting image is to use lines going across a stripe to divide it up. By experimenting with colours and changing the length of the sections and the width of the stripe, you can achieve very different effects. This is a good way of using up odd pieces of wool. It is also fascinating because every time you finish a stripe you have to make a decision about the next one. As you make these decisions you develop your skill in picturing the final outcome.

You can also use another shape within the stripe, changing its size as each stripe is worked. The shape could be a geometric one, such as a star, or a more organic one, such as a flower head. It's fun, too, to experiment with colours in these designs. Try using startling shades in small quantities and experiment by juxtaposing colours you would not

Fig. 22 Different ways of repeating a square. The squares can be joined together or have spaces between them

decided, the placing of stitches is a simple matter of counting. This makes the task a relaxing one, which can be picked up and resumed easily after a break. (Although you do have to count carefully. It is not relaxing to discover that a large area of stitching has to be undone

70

normally put together. This sometimes produces a surprising richness. (See Chapter 5 for more about colour.)

ADDING INTEREST

Be careful that your repetitive design does not become boring. Using too few colours can result in a pattern with no visual interest. Too much predictability can be tedious both to look at and to work. There are lots of ways to add spice to a simple design. For instance:

☐ Vary the texture within the shapes by using tones, as in Project 2 (p. 21), or by using textured stitches.

☐ Stretch the design out or squash it up.

☐ Use the patchwork technique of dividing the design into strips and moving them up and down to produce a more interesting image (see fig. 23).

☐ Patterns can be used very successfully to texture an area within a pictorial design. They can also be used to create a border or to fill connecting areas in a design.

☐ Light and dark areas in a pattern can create a visual illusion. You may know the Heavenly Steps patchwork design, which is made from light, medium and dark rhombuses and squares. This three-dimensional effect can be

Stripes don't have to be boring. These were worked with odd scraps of wool

71

Right: A surprising corner in an otherwise uninteresting design enlivens the whole thing. (We hope you have to look hard to notice the change in the colour of the background. This is what can happen if you run out of a colour halfway through a design. Although it was supposed to be the same shade, the wool was not the same dye lot)

achieved on canvas relatively easily. Different colours and textures may be included for added interest, provided the light, medium and dark tones are maintained throughout.

□ Another way of adding visual interest is to 'peep' through from one pattern to another. Leave holes in your first pattern and fill them with another as if it was showing through from underneath. Used sparingly, this intriguing device can be very successful in enlivening an all-over design. The placing of the peep-holes is crucial and you will need to experiment, perhaps with paper cut-outs, to get it right.

□ This final point is one we have made already, but it bears repetition. Unusual colour combinations can help to achieve an interesting effect.

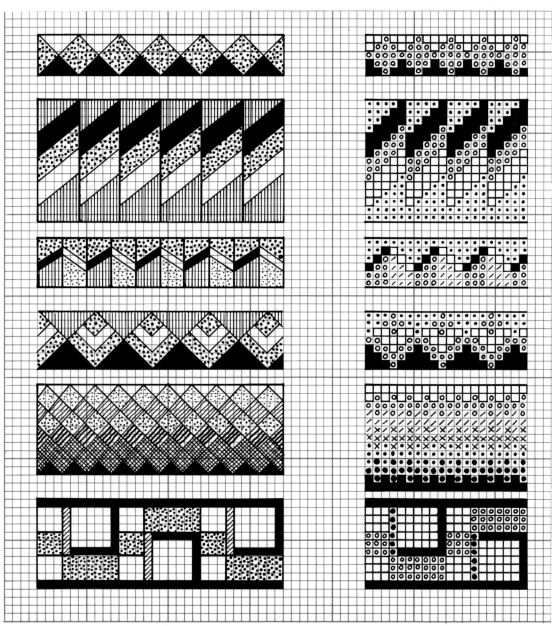

Fig. 23 *The patterned stripes of Seminole patchwork can be adapted for stitching on canvas. In the column on the right, each symbol represents a different tone or colour*

Far left: *In this piece you look through windows in one design to another behind it*

Patterns are very good for linking colours in a room and can look spectacular en masse. Once you have begun, it is difficult to stop.

Beware!

We have already warned you that needlepoint can become addictive.

Stitching patterns is particularly so. The 'I'll just do that bit before I go to bed' syndrome will rob you of sleep. The hypnotic rhythm of stitching a repeated shape, and the accompanying thought processes ('I wonder whether a touch of slime green would bring this to life?'), will kill conversation.

73

SUPER STRIPES

This project does not require you to make many decisions before you begin to stitch, but it will let you practise the design skill of making frequent choices as your work progresses.

Create a design by putting a simple shape, such as a triangle, inside a stripe. If you do not want to use an angular shape, try a curved one instead. Think about the spaces around the shapes as well as the shapes themselves. Are you going to make the background stripe a single colour, or work around each shape in a different colour?

Stitch one stripe first, then work the next one to a different width. Each time you finish a stripe, decide how wide to make the following one. Use as many colours as possible in your design and experiment with some you don't normally use.

Super Stripes

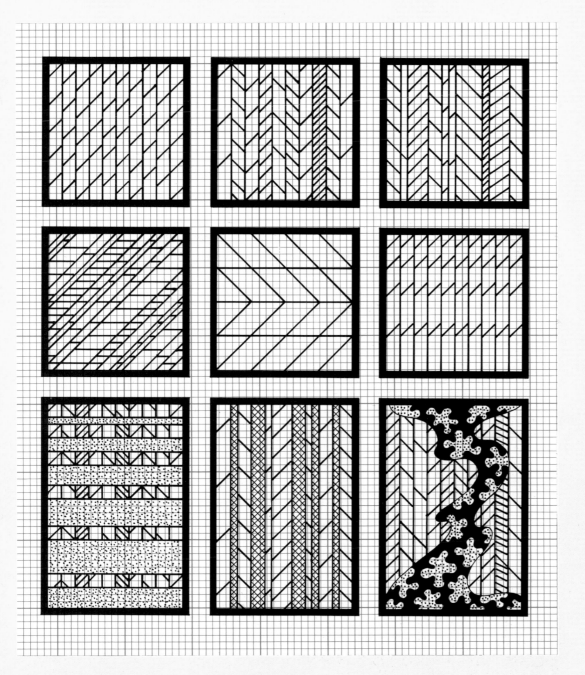

Fig. 24 Different ways of dividing stripes into parallelograms

CHAPTER 8

MAKING CONNECTIONS

How many different ways can you think of to use a brick? Psychologists sometimes test ingenuity by asking this question, and people come up with the most amazing lists. It seems that a simple but somewhat bizarre exercise can spark off an extraordinary variety of thoughts if the mind is allowed to explore new connections. We have certainly found that one idea leads to another where needlepoint is involved. Sometimes the connecting thought is obvious. For example, a carved picture frame, found in an antique shop, featured leaves and snakes, and cried out for an Adam and Eve design to fill it.

Inspired by the frame, this picture has a knitted background. It is not needlepoint, but could equally well have been designed as such

SEEING POSSIBILITIES

Sometimes connections are less obvious and discoveries are made almost by mistake. A half-finished coloured geometric design reminded us of lace and looked very pretty. This prompted the idea of painting canvas with a pale wash and working a white lacy pattern, leaving some of the canvas exposed. (The canvas was painted with oil-based paint thinned with white spirit. Care was taken in finishing off the threads while stitching, because it was important that no thread was seen behind the bare painted spaces.)

ABSTRACTING

Sometimes a whole chain of linked ideas comes from a single source. An attempt to stitch a design based on a photograph of flowers on the cover of *The Garden* magazine resulted in three pieces of needlepoint rather than one. The initial attraction of the picture was that the colours were striking and almost in conflict. There was precise definition in the foreground, coupled with a misty, unfocused background composed of blobs of colour almost thrown across the grass. The first idea was simply to try to reproduce the photograph in stitching. As the picture was worked, it was seen that the background could become abstract, with the small flowers gradually transformed into a pattern that would mingle with the spiky shapes of the tall

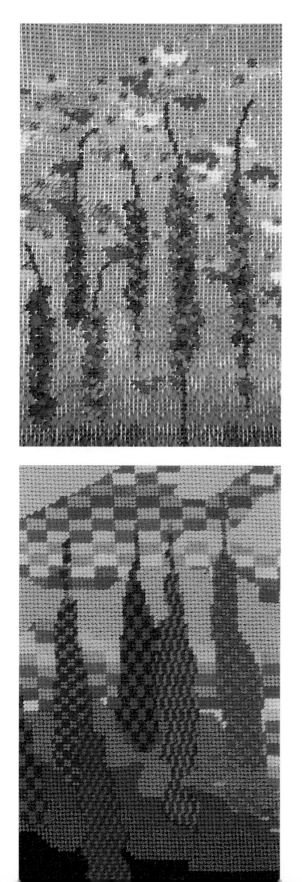

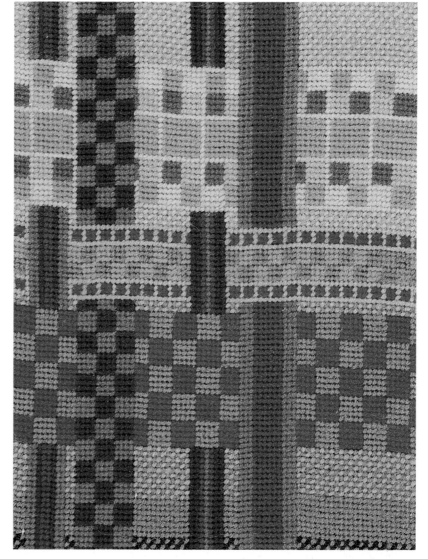

mauve flowers. Eventually a third version developed, based on embroidered ribbons weaving in and out, an impression created by the photograph. These interwoven ribbons of colour emerged again in a different piece of work (see p. 92). Ideas do recur, often unconsciously, in different designs.

Three versions of a design taken from the cover of The Garden *magazine*

77

Jennie's finished quilt. It won first prize at the UK *National Patchwork Championships in* 1992, *and the prize for Best First Quilt at the American Quilter's Society Annual Show in* 1993

FOLLOWING TRAINS OF THOUGHT

Another whole sequence of ideas began when Jennie took up quilting. Her first patchwork quilt was multicoloured and made from samples of her batik work. She cut the patches and tacked them over graph paper before sewing them together.

78

Gradually block upon block of colour was added, and as the quilt grew it became increasingly unwieldy and the paper crackled when it was moved. Jennie sat for many hours with the quilt draped over her lap as she stitched. In this position she was often looking at the back of the work as well as at the more solid colour of the front. She became fascinated by the views of the underside, the mixture of neat but free colouring and the pale, rigid shapes of the graph paper edged with little strips of frayed fabric. She

Far left: *The back of the quilt with the papers intact*

Left: *Collage of photographs taken from both sides of the finished quilt*

photographed both the front and the back of the quilt and made a collage of the photographs. This was the basis for a needlepoint design, and she learned a lot by trying to reproduce the luminous dappled colours of the quilt in woollen stitches. She looked at the canvas a great deal, both as she worked and after she had finished it, and became particularly attracted to one part of the design. She decided to use this intriguing area again, working it on a much larger scale to make a rug.

INTEGRATING YOUR SURROUNDINGS

Many connections are much more down to earth than these experiments. They are made for practical reasons when we are creating something to fit into a particular room and to unify a motley collection of furniture and furnishings. For instance, you can use the colours already printed on the material of a sofa and add those in the carpet, in the surround of the fireplace or in ornaments around the room. You may dream of having new

79

This design, inspired by the quilt in the photograph on p. 78, was worked mostly in crewel wool so that the colours could be mixed with strands of very light tones. In addition, some of the whiteness of the canvas was allowed to show through to create a light effect similar to that of the dyes used to make the quilt

curtains only to find, when you finally get them, that they dominate the room and spoil everything else. We have stitched cushions and pictures to rescue such a situation, and managed to change the balance of colour and pattern in a room to help highlight similarities rather than accentuate differences. Choosing those aspects of the existing decor that you particularly like as a basis for your own design helps to make the whole more pleasing. You can use motifs from a floor covering to stitch something for the wall or, conversely, use part of a poster hanging above a mantelpiece as a design for a hearthrug.

Left: When new, this
rug dominated the room

Below: This quite large
(50 cm square)
needlepoint design, hung
over the mantelpiece,
subdued the rug. The
shading across it was
included to add visual
interest

HAVING CONFIDENCE

There are people who say that they
cannot produce ideas of their own. We
find this difficult to believe. Everyone has
inventive thoughts but some people have
a lot more confidence than others. The
only way to gain confidence in your ideas
is to try them out. Equally, there are other
people who have such lively imaginations
that their problem is to make decisions,
to stop making connections and to settle
down to make something. Sometimes
people get stuck in a rut and keep
producing work based on one idea, which
can become repetitive and predictable.
Ideally you need enough confidence to try
new ideas, to recognise failures and
accept them as useful learning
experiences, and to move on to tackle
new flights of fancy.

PROJECT EIGHT

ZOOM IN

This project will encourage you to develop your own design from an image you already like. Find a photograph, postcard or fabric sample that interests you. Cut a hole 4 cm (1½ in) square out of an A4-sized piece of paper or card. Move this peep-hole around on top of your chosen image to find part of it to sew. You are choosing a composition that particularly pleases you. It may well look like an abstract design, not a recognisable object.

Trace the outline of the main shapes within the peep-hole. Enlarge them to the size you want (see fig. 25) and draw them onto the canvas. Now that you have copied the chosen shapes, you can enjoy filling them in. You may want to add patterns and details that are not in the original.

Right: The peep-hole should be twisted around and moved up and down

Far right: Tulip design based on enlarged detail of photograph (left). The red parts of the design were the last to be worked. An attempt was made to connect them using line and shading

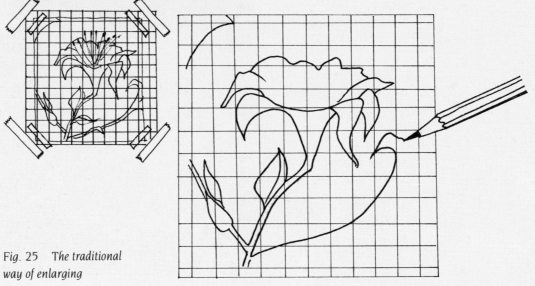

Fig. 25   *The traditional way of enlarging*

82

CHAPTER 9

MAKING IT PERSONAL

When you create your own designs you can personalise your work in a way that is not possible with commercially produced kits. We have had great fun making presents for friends and family, and their interests have inspired designs and given us ideas we would never have thought of otherwise.

IDENTIFYING AN INTEREST

☐ Heinz is passionately interested in music. At the age of eighty he discovered a quartet in the British Library which he believed was written by Mozart, although it had not previously been attributed to the composer. He had a marvellous time

Mozart quartet in E flat major for piano, violin, viola and cello

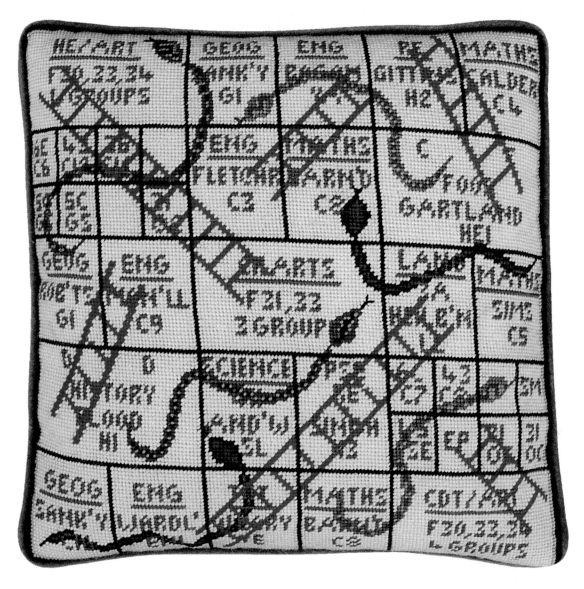

researching this exciting find and proving his case. The cushion made for him as a Christmas present featured part of the score of the quartet worked over faint Mozart silhouettes. The music was quite difficult to copy. It is important, if you make a present for an expert, to get the technical details as correct as possible. A musical friend helped to interpret the score and the silhouette was traced from a photograph of a bust of Mozart.

□ Phil teaches in a large inner-city comprehensive school and has the unenviable task of drawing up the school timetable each summer. This is a lengthy and complicated job – as soon as one problem is solved, another emerges. Spirits rise only to be dashed again. This idea inspired a cushion showing part of the timetable overlaid by a pattern of snakes and ladders.

Opposite: An attempt to make needlepoint look like knitting. An alternative would be to knit a piece and apply it to the canvas

☐ Jane is a keen knitter. A cushion was made for her, using the colours of her new chair and celebrating her hobby. It featured stitches that looked like knitting. The balls of wool were made of lengths of thread couched onto the background. The needles were padded by laying the wool along the canvas in very long straight stitches and then stitching over it. This technique is called tramming.

☐ Stefanie's father was an engineer who was brought up in Cornwall. A picture made for her commemorates her first visit to the north Cornish coast, where she was fascinated by the old tin mines and their impact on the landscape.

☐ A house that was once a chapel has been Ruth's family home for more than fifty years. It was quite easy to sew a picture of it on canvas as most of the shapes were so simple.

The ruined tin mines on the Cornish coast are very dark compared with the surrounding countryside

☐ Another idea for a personalised gift is to buy two photograph frames and put a detail of a photo in one and an embroidery of the same image, sewn on canvas, in the other. Such small pieces (which may be 4–5 cm or 2 in across) are quick to do, but test your ingenuity.

RESEARCHING YOUR DESIGN

The art of making a personal present involves real knowledge of the person who will receive it. It is essential to hit the right note and produce something that gives pleasure rather than embarrassment. To do this requires observation and thought, and may take a lot of research if you are to get the details correct. Most people have a particular interest such as sport, gardening, opera, film, cars, fashion, stamp collecting, local history or cooking, and you need to know something about it if you are to create a design for them. For instance, a loyal football fan may have seen his team play in a cup final, a collector may have been searching for a particular stamp for years, an opera buff may have saved the money to see all of Wagner's Ring cycle. Your designs can celebrate such achievements as well as more obvious events such as birthdays, weddings or anniversaries.

Such a personal approach to design presents particular challenges. Stitching a rare stamp is technically quite difficult and will require careful preliminary

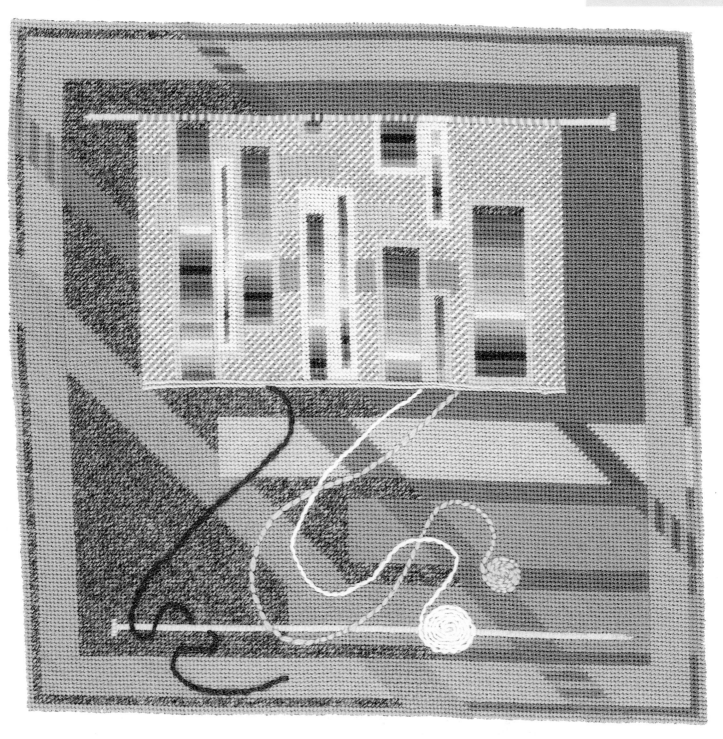

The simple outlines of this house were traced by placing a photograph underneath the canvas

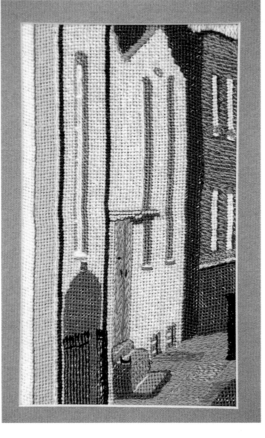

research. This may be complicated, especially if the finished gift is to be a surprise and you cannot consult the 'expert'.

PRESENTATION

We always try to finish our work to as high a standard as possible. It is no use spending hours stitching a wonderful piece of needlepoint and then leaving it crooked and crumpled. It will need to be stretched accurately, and should be dampened thoroughly and nailed out on a board (see p. 94). To ensure that a rectangular piece is accurately stretched, measure the diagonals: they should be equal. If you are not confident about stretching work yourself, it may be worth the expense of getting it done professionally. Most embroidery shops offer such a service. It is also possible to buy a machine that makes the task simple; it could be a good investment if you are going to do a lot of work. You could share the cost of one with a friend. The address of the manufacturer is given on p. 95 of this book.

Cushions, once stretched, are best piped and backed with a fairly heavy material. The work itself is thick and needs an equally firm backing. We usually use velvet, largely because it is the right weight and is available in many beautiful colours. It is worth looking out for remnants in sales and discount fabric shops. Feather cushions are more comfortable than those filled with artificial fibre, and you will need to buy one that is at least 2 or 3 cm (1 in) bigger than the cover if you want it to remain firm.

Rugs are best hemmed after stretching, and backed with a strong flat fabric. This helps to keep them in shape but it does have a disadvantage. Pieces of grit and dirt can fall through the rug and be trapped by the backing, rubbing against it and wearing it out.

Needlepoint pictures also need to be stretched and can be framed or mounted over a piece of strong card or plywood.

With care you can produce presents that will give pleasure for years to come.

PROJECT NINE

A GREETINGS CARD

Craft shops sell cards that can be used to frame embroideries. Choose one, or make one yourself. With the shape and colour of the frame in mind, embroider a greetings card for someone you know well. Try to make the design personal to them. You will not have much space, so you will have to think carefully about what to include.

Right: Clare, aged seven, stitched a portrait of her pet rabbit as an Easter card. The background was coloured with various felt-tip pens

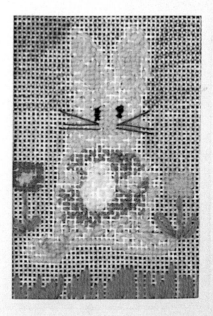

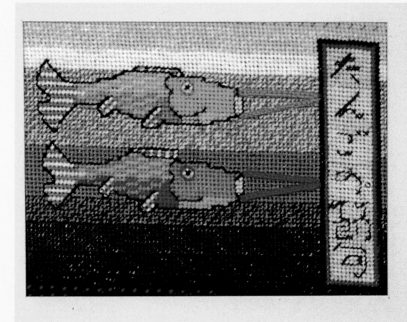

Above: A card to mark Japanese Boys' Day, made for a Japanese family who had two small sons

Right: Hilary's fortieth birthday was to be celebrated by a trip to picturesque Venice

CHAPTER 10

BEING YOURSELF

A graphologist can tell a lot about you by studying your handwriting; apparently it reflects your personality and experience. An artist's work shows a progression but, although it matures and develops, it also has an identifiable and individual style which remains consistent. When you work a design on canvas your personality is reflected both in what you choose to sew and the way you choose to do it. It is important to know yourself and how your personality affects your work. For instance, you may realise that your patience is short-lived and therefore it might be best to choose projects you can finish quickly, before your patience runs out, using large-gauge canvas or making relatively small pieces. Alternatively, you may be aware that you are obsessive about some things, such as the type of materials you use or the way in which you go about your needlepoint, and that these habits are hindering the development of your craft. Sometimes making do with a thread or canvas that is not quite what you had in mind will prove to be a really successful move.

We know each other's work well and have sat stitching together on many occasions, but the process of writing this book has made us examine our individual differences. Examples of our work are included throughout the book, but we have not put our names to them. As you read the following self-appraisals you might like to try to guess who made what. (The answers can be found in the Appendix on p. 95.)

ANN

I am quite logical. I like trying new ideas but I usually experiment a bit first before I begin. I tend to do representational designs using people, flowers and animals, rather than abstract patterns. I am not at all confident about drawing and think my work often looks naive and childish. I usually have to research my designs carefully and copy or trace the shapes I need. I think that I like soft and subdued colours, but in fact most of my work is quite bright and I tend to use primary rainbow colours a lot. I like order and progression and have used some themes, e.g. the four seasons, repeatedly. I have always enjoyed experimenting with a variety of stitches and threads. I usually use relatively large-gauge canvas. I find initial decisions difficult, and work at them before allowing myself the relief of starting to stitch. I have done a lot of designs for family and friends. I like things that amuse me.

JENNIE

I am intuitive rather than logical. I love pattern, containment and the odd surprise. My work is controlled and although I would like to be freer I find this difficult. I enjoy drawing, as well as a variety of crafts, including batik, quilting and knitting. I have a disregard for conventional colour rules and love experimenting with unusual mixtures. I have an aggressive streak. I plan designs in my head and often start stitching without a great deal of preparation. I have very high levels of patience and perseverance. I like my work to be smooth and even, and prefer working with 12- or 14-gauge canvas so that I can get the detail I require. I prefer not to use textured threads, but to produce the illusion of texture by the use of colour and pattern. In recent years my house has been refurbished and I have enjoyed making pictures, cushions and rugs for it.

YOUR STYLE

The fact that you choose to express yourself through needlepoint rather than some other art form probably says something about your personality. The constraints it imposes are, in a way, very reassuring and safe. It is an adult version of the Binca embroidery you did at primary school.

Rather than suggesting a single project for Chapter 10, we have decided to conclude the book with ten ideas to start you on your way. Have fun doing your own thing!

Our mothers hate this portrait of us, but stitching it was fun. We do smile sometimes!

91

IDEAS FOR PROJECTS

□ Try an aerial view. Imagine somewhere you know well (a garden, a nearby street, a swimming pool, a lake, a farm, a kitchen, the inside of a local library or supermarket) seen from above. Alternatively, you could draw inspiration from a book of aerial photographs (see p. 95).

□ Stitch a window and what you see through it, either from the inside looking out or the outside looking in.

□ Use two different colourways of variegated double knitting wool to make a geometric design, one colourway for the pattern and the other for the background. This is relatively inexpensive (you need only two balls of knitting wool rather than a lot of skeins of tapestry wool) and interesting to do, because you cannot tell at first what the changing colours in the wool will look like when they are worked in a design.

□ Work a design showing the four seasons. You could use people in seasonal clothing, hedgerows, trees, fields – any image that will change as the seasons do.

□ Consider the visual impact of other types of embroidery (e.g. blackwork patterns on a white or coloured background). How could you translate this into needlepoint?

□ Use a simple flower shape, e.g. a geranium, fuchsia or wild rose. Cover the canvas with these flowers worked in different colours. You can put leaves between the flower shapes if you wish.

□ Experiment with different types of canvas. Plastic canvas can be used to make three-dimensional decorations for a festival such as Christmas. Try working a logo on a tee shirt using waste canvas. Remove the canvas by wetting it and pulling out the threads when you have finished stitching.

□ Create a design for a dance enthusiast, a weight-watcher, a bridge player, a computer-games addict or someone who has just passed their driving test. Make it personal!

□ Try a picture of a house, your own or someone else's. Have fun with the details.

□ If you have access to a computer-graphics package, try using it to transform a motif from a rug pattern into a design for a cushion or vice versa. A computer can easily repeat a pattern for you and rotate or reverse it.

Design derived from an antique piece of Mola work

A PPENDIX

USEFUL TECHNIQUES

ENLARGING A DESIGN

There are several ways of doing this.

- ☐ The traditional way explained in Project 8, p. 82.
- ☐ Using a photocopier. This is more expensive but very quick. Most machines will provide various degrees of enlargement, and if you like to work from a chart you can try photocopying directly onto graph paper.
- ☐ Using an overhead projector. Trace or draw your design onto clear acetate, project it onto a sheet of paper on the wall and outline the projected image. The farther the projector is from the wall the bigger the enlargement will be.

TRANSFERRING A DESIGN ON TO CANVAS

Different ways of transferring a design serve different purposes but most people have a favourite method. We often trace directly onto the canvas using a pencil (see fig. 26), but if a complicated design needs clear definition we use a fine permanent marker. If you use such a marker, leave the ink to dry thoroughly before you begin to stitch. Some people paint their designs onto canvas with thinned oil paint. Whatever you use to mark the canvas, it is important to choose a colour that is dark enough to see, but won't show through pale wool stitching.

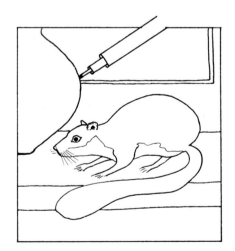

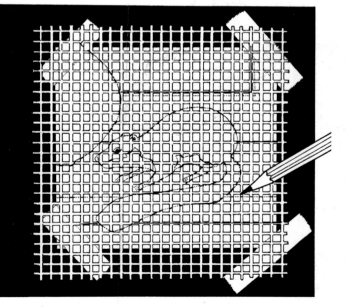

Fig. 26   The simplest way of transferring a design on to canvas

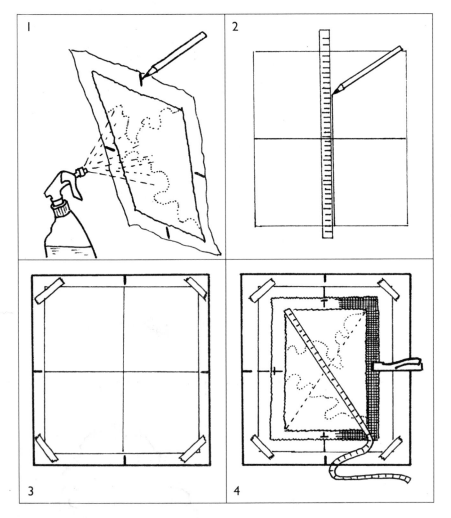

Fig. 27   How to stretch a canvas

1 Mark the centre point on each side of the canvas. Spray thoroughly with water.

2 Take a piece of paper slightly larger than the needlepoint design, but smaller than the wooden board on which it is to be stretched. Mark accurate lines down and across the middle.

3 Mark the centre point of each side of the board. Attach the paper with masking tape, matching the centre points.

4 Using a staple gun (or tacks), attach the canvas to the board, starting at the centre points. Pull and shape the rest of the work and staple it. To check that it is rectangular, measure the diagonals. They should be equal.

STRETCHING FINISHED WORK

Here again, everyone seems to have a favourite method. We have bought a stretching machine, which is very easy and quick to use. The address of the manufacturer can be found on p. 95. You need to be fairly prolific to make such a purchase worthwhile, but we have found it invaluable. Fig. 27 shows a reliable method of getting good results without a machine.

MATERIALS

Plastic mesh is available for small pieces of work. It is sold in a variety of colours and gauges. Special wools (thicker than tapestry wool) can also be obtained for use with it. The advantage of using plastic canvas is that you can make three-dimensional objects such as boxes. Because the mesh does not fray and is rigid when worked, it can be cut to shape and pieces can be joined by overstitching. The disadvantage is that you have to sew carefully. If you pull too hard on a stitch the mesh will break.

Paper mesh, made of thin coloured card, is also available and is useful for making greetings cards and Christmas decorations.

FURTHER READING

Bradkin, Cheryl Greider, *Basic Seminole Patchwork*, Leone, 1990

Seminole patterns to adapt for needlepoint

Ehrman, Hugh, and Benn, Elizabeth, *Noah's Ark: Animals in Needlepoint*, Century, 1989

Contains designs for Pansy the cow and many other animals

Fassett, Kaffe, *Glorious Needlepoint*, Century, 1987

Designs include Kabuki face

Gerster, George, *Grand Design: The Earth from Above*, Paddington Press, 1977

A collection of aerial views. This book is really worth tracking down

Gross, Nancy D., and Fontana, Frank, *Shisha Embroidery: Traditional Indian Mirror Work*, Dover, 1981

Shisha designs and instructions for attaching mirrors

Higginson, Susan, *The Book of Needlepoint Stitches*, A. & C. Black, 1989

Contains instructions for working a wide range of stitches

Seward, Linda, *The Complete Book of Patchwork, Quilting, and Appliqué*, Mitchell Beazley, 1987

Patchwork patterns to adapt for needlepoint

50 Canvas Embroidery Stitches, Coats Patons Crafts

Collections of stitches from a leading manufacturer

EQUIPMENT SUPPLIERS

R and R Enterprises
13 Frederick Road
Malvern Link
Worcestershire
WR14 1RS

Embroidery frames made from plastic tubing

Easy-Stretch
40 New Odiham Road
Alton
Hampshire
GU34 1QG

Stretching machines (will supply worldwide)

WHO MADE WHAT?

The designs on pp. 9, 11, 28, 31, 32, 35, 36, 37, 42, 44, 63, 66, 67, 68, 71, 72, 78, 79, 80, 81, 86, 89, 91 and 92 are by Jennie Petersen.

All other designs are by Ann Gittins, with the exception of the rabbit worked by Clare Gittins (p. 89).

INDEX